The Death of Religion

The Dor Series, Volume 1

Genesis Joyner

Published by Genesis Joyner, 2021.

THE DEATH OF RELIGION

First edition. September 18, 2021.

ISBN: 979-8201402273

Written by Genesis Joyner.

Table of Contents

Dedicated to those that are waking up. Slumber no more...

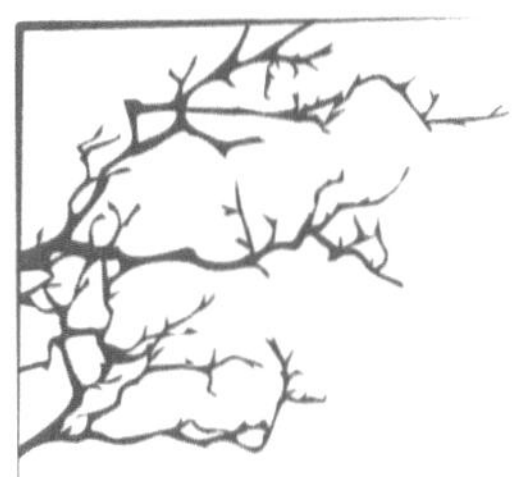

Shout Outs

I want to thank God, Jesus, and the Holy Spirit for saving my life. I am nothing without you and I love you.

I want to thank everyone everywhere for being a part of this book. All of my life experiences have played a role in moving forward and showing what I have learned to help others. I know you didn't know you were helping me with this decision but thank you.

I want to thank my mom for believing in me.

I want to thank God, Jesus, and the Holy Spirit for saving my life. I am nothing without you and I love you.

I want to thank Marlo @ The Magnuson Hotel. You my boo and yo know why:) When I am in a better situation. I got you fam. I love you sis. Couldn't have done this without your help.

I want to thank The Black King Midas. My true friend. "We just got to get there!" Jumbrella Foreva - GWhizz

I want to thank Tyshenna and Aminah - I appreciate all the invested time. May God heal all wounds and make all whole in Jesus name. Love you.

My Aunt Magi - Man the jewels that you have given me were awesome. What I appreciate most is you encouraging me to own me, love me, express me, even when it's not popular. I love you very much.

To the Body of Christ it is time to rise up. Ask the hard questions and keep asking until you get the answers. We have been deceived. Let's glow in the dark.

My children - Destiny, Trinity, Serenity, and Sincere. You are some of the most amazing human beings that I have ever met. Forgiving, loving, kind, funny. I learned how to smile again because of who you are. It's not for nothing. Everything that God said He is going to do He is going to do. I love you in Jesus name. You are more to me than children you are brothers and sisters in Christ. You are vibrant souls! Never leave the path of God He will never let you down!

Future Hubby - Where you at boo? Lol! I guess I have to thank you for taking your time. Yo you didn't want me before the conversion, straight up :)

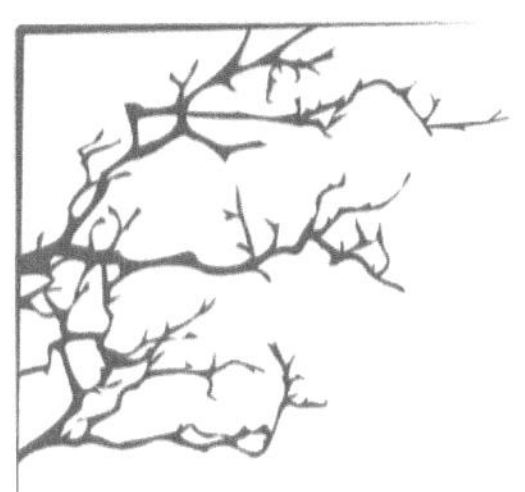

Prayer

Dear Heavenly Father,
My prayer is simple. Please God forgive me for my sins. I repent for all things that I have ever done that give you a bad name. I spent a lot of time in the enemies camp. I owe you my life. You saved it so I give it to you.

I pray that you call your seed to arms. That you, through this series will empower us to seek you. I pray that you let your children (even those that do not know they are your children) have ears to hear, eyes to see, and a heart to repent. I pray that you get us tuned in to your voice. For the sheep only respond to the voice of the Shepherd. I pray that you send harvesters. I pray that souls are saved and lives are changed. Finally I pray that people will stop searching for healing and start seeking you for wholeness. Those are not the same things. I pray Lord that people will see the value in these words in Jesus name and never turn back. God I ask finally for your will to be done on earth as it is in heaven. Really there is no other way. I love you. Let's get it in Jesus name I make my request known. Amen!

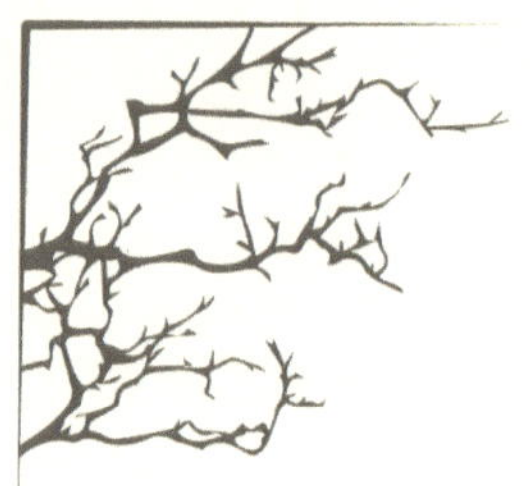

Drum Roll Please

Why this book? To be honest it's because God said so! I know how that sounds. You are probably thinking everyone says that. Or maybe you're thinking "is she being sarcastic?". In all seriousness it's a mix of both. I am writing this because obedience to God is better than sacrifice (enter appropriate scripture) and it has its reward (enter other popular scripture). It is also because I originally didn't want to write it (enter sarcasm filled with all truth). This book will be different from other books you have read only because God is using me to write this one. I'm pretty sure this will be the first in a volume because it's really just a log of discussions thoughts and lessons that we all go through on this journey. Things that I wish I had known when I began this journey to please God and to live with Him forever..

With that being said there has been a change. I am now very excited about writing this book for a few reasons. First reason being I learn when I teach (find scriptures supporting that). Another reason is because it's a book about things I am actually interested in. It will cover things that I feel kept me from following Christ effectively sooner. Let me give an example.

Have you ever put an address in the GPS? Maybe you had somewhere important to get to so you did your due diligence in looking the night before. You wake up in the appropriate amount of time (based upon information that you researched because what the heck doesn't google know, right?) ! Get dressed, eat, and brush teeth feeling confident. Time of arrival to said interview, wedding , dinner, or funeral is 27 minutes. Traffic is faster than usual.

Have you ever had that type of confidence? When you know that you absolutely did everything right, at least you think so. Okay back to the story. You get 10 minutes into your trip. Your music is jamming and you are excited about what lies ahead in the future. Except you find that the street that you need, the exit that you want, the end you desire is blocked or not in sight. You don't initially panic (no not you) because you know without a shadow of a doubt that your faithful GPS that has been programmed by man is without error (or closer to perfect than most things). You continue to follow what the GPS tells you as you reroute and remain calm. But then something else happens; its starts raining and not just any rain it's heavy rain. This is so weird because you also checked the weather last night and it said no chance of rain ever, ever, ever, forever, never!

As a result of this unexpected rain you find that the traffic that was said to be faster than usual is now slow as I don't know what. Now my friend... you are nervous. Even with all your planning you are late to your major event. It's true... you did all you could, but there was an error in the system in which you learned and as a result you showed up late! Well, that's how I feel about Christianity. Well, at least my experience because you will learn that I don't talk about you I talk about me.

(Insert professional intro) Hello my name is Genesis Joyner. I am the co-founder of Vizion Injneering. God is the founder! We believe in bringing people to Christ through love and transparency. I tell my story hoping that it will help you along the way. So let's dig into this. By the way, this is not a book like other books. Prepare for beautiful realism accompanied by unprofessional-ism. Okay start again...(add dramatic music) Chapter 1 is called "The sweet decision in the valley of Jehoshaphat."

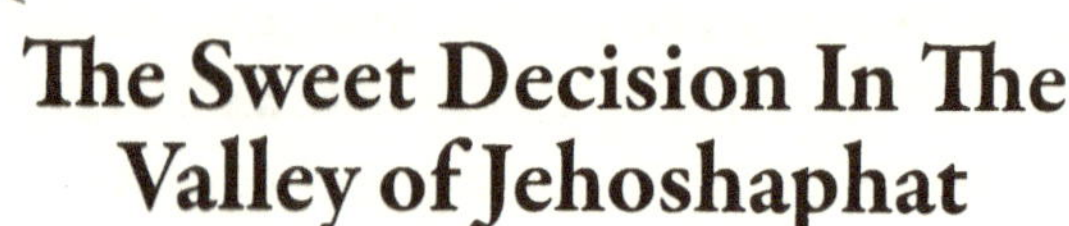

The Sweet Decision In The Valley of Jehoshaphat

In Joel Chapter 3 (the king new international living translation) of the bible. There are two things that really stick out to me. The first is the term the Valley of Jehoshaphat. It's a place that the Lord announced he was having a meeting at. He invited his frenemies as he was pretty bothered at how they had treated his kids. The term Valley of Jehoshaphat means God has judged. He tells them some of the things he is ticked off at. In short you will find if you read that he is pretty angry about the whole ordeal. I would leave you to sort that thing out on your own with reading it and all, but I would rather assume you don't have a bible, or don't know how to read, or don't want to read it on your own. Therefore I will insert the verses here for you. Because if you are anything like I was you don't really feel like leaving the book you actually like to go and read the bible (enter conviction, fire, and brimstone lol).

3 "For, behold, in those days, and in that time, when I shall bring again the captivity of Judah and Jerusalem,

2 I will also gather all nations, and will bring them down into the valley of Jehoshaphat, and will plead with them there for my people and for my heritage Israel, whom they have scattered among the nations, and parted my land.

3 And they have cast lots for my people; and have given a boy for an harlot, and sold a girl for wine, that they might drink.

4 Yea, and what have ye to do with me, O Tyre, and Zidon, and all the coasts of Palestine? will ye render me a recompence? and if ye recompense me, swiftly and speedily will I return your recompence upon your own head;

5 Because ye have taken my silver and my gold, and have carried into your temples my goodly pleasant things:

6 The children also of Judah and the children of Jerusalem have ye sold unto the Grecians, that ye might remove them far from their border.

7 Behold, I will raise them out of the place whither ye have sold them, and will return your recompence upon your own head:

8 And I will sell your sons and your daughters into the hand of the children of Judah, and they shall sell them to the Sabeans, to a people far off: for the Lord hath spoken it.

9 Proclaim ye this among the Gentiles; Prepare war, wake up the mighty men, let all the men of war draw near; let them come up:

10 Beat your plowshares into swords and your pruninghooks into spears: let the weak say, I am strong.

11 Assemble yourselves, and come, all ye heathen, and gather yourselves together round about: thither cause thy mighty ones to come down, O Lord.

12 Let the heathen be wakened, and come up to the valley of Jehoshaphat: for there will I sit to judge all the heathen round about." Joel 3:1-12 King James Version (KJV)

I don't know if you read what I read, but in addition to being bothered by His own kids acting out God is also holding the people who influenced them and took advantage of their lack of knowledge responsible as well. This Valley of Jehoshaphat then becomes the Valley of Decision in verse 14. Don't worry I have that verse for you too (wink wink)!

"14 Multitudes, multitudes in the valley of decision: for the day of the Lord is near in the valley of decision." King James Version (KJV)

Here's the thing that I wish we all understood. The Lord really has no respect of persons. That means he has no favorites. Like seriously! It's no mistake that the place of God's Judgement is also called the Valley of Decision even though they are both the same place. Have you ever watched someone else get in trouble? What about when you know you have done the same thing when you knew better? It's a scary kind of feeling, right? It's also the very feeling that we need to begin to pay attention to. It's called conviction.

33 "But this shall be the covenant that I will make with the house of Israel; After those days, saith the Lord, I will put my law in their inward

parts, and write it in their hearts; and will be their God, and they shall be my people." Jeremiah 31:33 King James Version (KJV)

It's the Lord's way of telling us that we know right from wrong. It's the Lord's way of telling us that it's time to repent and that we are indeed guilty. It is also God's way of telling us that He loves us.

6 "For whom the Lord loves He chastens, And scourges every son whom He receives.

7 If you endure chastening, God deals with you as with sons; for what son is there whom a father does not chasten?

8 But if you are without chastening, of which all have become partakers, then you are illegitimate and not sons.

9 Furthermore, we have had human fathers who corrected us, and we paid them respect. Shall we not much more readily be in subjection to the Father of spirits and live?

10 For they indeed for a few days chastened us as seemed best to them, but He for our profit, that we may be partakers of His holiness.

11 Now no chastening seems to be joyful for the present, but painful; nevertheless, afterward it yields the peaceable fruit of righteousness to those who have been trained by it." Hebrews 12:6-11 New King James Version (NKJV)

Yes, God was upset about how his children were treated. However, He was also angry at how the children had allowed themselves to be treated. He was angry at how they had treated Him in the process. The bottom line is everyone was being judged."

10 "For we must all appear before the judgment seat of Christ; that every one may receive the things done in his body, according to that he hath done, whether it be good or bad." 2 Corinthians 5:10 King James Version (KJV)

Take the time right now to realize that at this moment as you read this handbook you are in the Valley of Jehoshaphat. Here, right now! God is bringing to remembrance the transgressions of others as an example for you to make a different choice in the Valley of Decision. It is important to know that when this life is all over that we will all end up in the place of judgment. Let us thank God for the ability to choose now so that we don't suffer later.

15 "And if it seem evil unto you to serve the Lord, choose you this day whom ye will serve; whether the gods which your fathers served that were on the other side of the flood, or the gods of the Amorites, in whose land ye dwell: but as for me and my house, we will serve the Lord." Joshua 24:15 King James Version (KJV)

Now that we have addressed this on a collective level, this is one of the things that I wish I would have understood as a new follower of Christ. God is doing things individually in our lives so that we can come together as a bride without blemish collectively. What do I mean by that? Did you notice that in Joel Chapter 3 some of the things that God mentioned that He didn't like we are doing and experiencing globally. For example,

"I will also gather all nations, and will bring them down into the valley of Jehoshaphat, and will plead with them there for my people and for my heritage Israel, whom they have scattered among the nations, and parted my land." Joel 3:2 King James Version (KJV)

This sounds a lot like what happened with slavery (not only with Africans). This sounds like what happens with anyone who has been or was stolen from there land. This sounds like the story of anyone who was (or is) stripped of their human rights and made to move, turn over, foreclose. See this type of behavior can apply to one of the ten commandments that God spoke about dealing with coveting thy neighbor's land, or ox, or whatever is thy neighbors.

17 "Thou shalt not covet thy neighbour's house, thou shalt not covet thy neighbour's wife, nor his manservant, nor his maidservant, nor his ox, nor his ass, nor any thing that is thy neighbour's." Exodus 20:17 King James Version (KJV)

Not to mention the things that are stolen spiritually. People everywhere have experienced scattering and being parted and God is not pleased.

6 "My people are destroyed for lack of knowledge: because thou hast rejected knowledge, I will also reject thee, that thou shalt be no priest to me: seeing thou hast forgotten the law of thy God, I will also forget thy children." Hosea 4:6 King James Version (KJV)

Let's look again

3 "And they have cast lots for my people; and have given a boy for an harlot, and sold a girl for wine, that they might drink.

4 Yea, and what have ye to do with me, O Tyre, and Zidon, and all the coasts of Palestine? will ye render me a recompence? and if ye recompense me, swiftly and speedily will I return your recompence upon your own head;" Joel 3:3-4 King James Version (KJV)

Those verses from thousands of years ago are talking about something that is running rampant in our country and it is called sex trafficking. The act of selling human beings for entertainment or gain. This does not only happens to females but also males. This abomination is not only done by those who are high in what the world considers power.

This action is also being taken by people who are not considered powerful. Those that are seeking power through unrighteous gain. Those who are bound because they serve mammon and not God. Those who are addicted to drugs, alcohol, sex, or even attention. It doesn't stop there! We also sell ourselves out. Trading over our children for and to the enemy because of our own illness. Prostituting, stripping, getting naked and teaching this behavior as a means to survive when it is really just killing us.

5 "Because ye have taken my silver and my gold, and have carried into your temples my goodly pleasant things:

6 The children also of Judah and the children of Jerusalem have ye sold unto the Grecians, that ye might remove them far from their border." Joel 3: 5-6 King James Version (KJV)

What about the children that are for sale. We are selling those who are close to us and even those that we don't know for silver and gold. The point is these things that we deal with could not exist collectively if there weren't individuals that have these issues. We have to be alert! If Christ is coming back for the church can you truly see us being ready when He gets here? Do you see yourself being ready? I am talking about right now as you read this today. I wonder if you are. I ponder this because the truth is there are far too many educators who are in error to not be concerned about if we are hearing the correct message.

The truth is there is a reason God says for lack of knowledge my people perish. It isn't a cute or prideful way. to throw shade. It is and was the truth. We are eating from the tree of the knowledge. However we are spitting out the good part and gorging ourselves on the the evil part. When he says that the whole world has been deceived it's more than just saying. It is a clue into what we need to change. God tells us to be not of this world while we are in it.

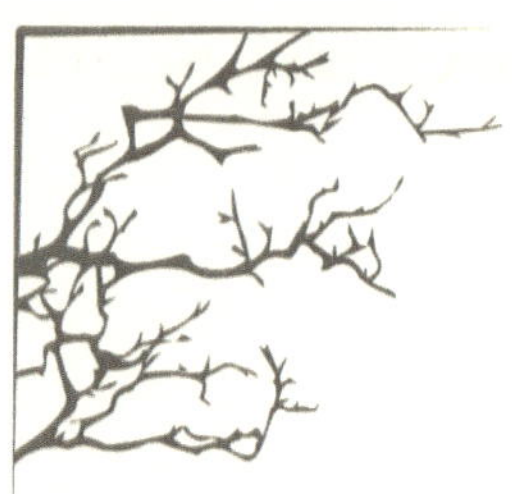

Deception

When you come out of the world you no longer have to be deceived.

2 "And be not conformed to this world: but be ye transformed by the renewing of your mind, that ye may prove what is that good, and acceptable, and perfect, will of God." Romans 12:2 King James Version (KJV)

Who are we learning from? When we come out of the world we get deceived because our educators have not come out the world yet. We don't know who is not deceived because we have been stripped of the tools needed to properly inspect fruit.

16 "Ye shall know them by their fruits. Do men gather grapes of thorns, or figs of thistles?

17 Even so every good tree bringeth forth good fruit; but a corrupt tree bringeth forth evil fruit.

18 A good tree cannot bring forth evil fruit, neither can a corrupt tree bring forth good fruit.

19 Every tree that bringeth not forth good fruit is hewn down, and cast into the fire.

20 Wherefore by their fruits ye shall know them." Matthew 7:16-20 King James Version (KJV)

When God is telling us that we will know them by their fruits what does He really mean? It is clear through media outlets and testimonies of people all over the world (the "church hurt"), that those who look like the "elect" are not following God and His heart's desires. Does a church full of members mean that there is good fruit? What about happy people in videos handing out food to the hungry? Does an event where the children can come out and enjoy one another give sufficient evidence of good fruit? I say no! In those same organizations there are families who are not being helped, scandals, indecent acts, favoritism, fornication, and much more.

5 "Then said he unto me, Son of man, lift up thine eyes now the way toward the north. So I lifted up mine eyes the way toward the north, and behold northward at the gate of the altar this image of jealousy in the entry.

6 He said furthermore unto me, Son of man, seest thou what they do? even the great abominations that the house of Israel committeth here, that I should go far off from my sanctuary? but turn thee yet again, and thou shalt see greater abominations.

7 And he brought me to the door of the court; and when I looked, behold a hole in the wall.

8 Then said he unto me, Son of man, dig now in the wall: and when I had digged in the wall, behold a door.

9 And he said unto me, Go in, and behold the wicked abominations that they do here.

10 So I went in and saw; and behold every form of creeping things, and abominable beasts, and all the idols of the house of Israel, pourtrayed upon the wall round about.

11 And there stood before them seventy men of the ancients of the house of Israel, and in the midst of them stood Jaazaniah the son of Shaphan, with every man his censer in his hand; and a thick cloud of incense went up.

12 Then said he unto me, Son of man, hast thou seen what the ancients of the house of Israel do in the dark, every man in the chambers of his imagery? for they say, the Lord seeth us not; the Lord hath forsaken the earth.

13 He said also unto me, Turn thee yet again, and thou shalt see greater abominations that they do.

14 Then he brought me to the door of the gate of the Lord's house which was toward the north; and, behold, there sat women weeping for Tammuz.

15 Then said he unto me, Hast thou seen this, O son of man? turn thee yet again, and thou shalt see greater abominations than these.

16 And he brought me into the inner court of the Lord's house, and, behold, at the door of the temple of the Lord, between the porch and the altar, were about five and twenty men, with their backs toward the temple

of the Lord, and their faces toward the east; and they worshipped the sun toward the east.

17 Then he said unto me, Hast thou seen this, O son of man? Is it a light thing to the house of Judah that they commit the abominations which they commit here? for they have filled the land with violence, and have returned to provoke me to anger: and, lo, they put the branch to their nose.

18 Therefore will I also deal in fury: mine eye shall not spare, neither will I have pity: and though they cry in mine ears with a loud voice, yet will I not hear them." Ezekiel 8: 5-18 King James Version (KJV)

We are talking about a word from God spoken thousands of years ago that still applies. Are those fruits that are good? Maybe you are saying sis you need to be promoting unity in the church. These are isolated incidents. If these are the exceptions that we should not judge then why is this so common in the "church"? What keeps us from correcting this few incidents? Could it be religious misinterpretation of what God spoke? Could it be intimidation through indoctrination? Maybe you feel like you saying that there is error in how things are being done means that you are sinning against God? Maybe someone told you that loving correction was the same as harming one of God's anointed.

22 "Saying, Touch not mine anointed, and do my prophets no harm." 1 Chronicles 16:22 King James Version (KJV)

Just maybe you heard that verse and were taught that standing against gross error was somehow against God's will. Maybe you were taught to believe that God appointed these leaders and educators and therefore they can do no wrong.

20 "For I say unto you, That except your righteousness shall exceed the righteousness of the scribes and Pharisees, ye shall in no case enter into the kingdom of heaven." Matthew 5:20 King James Version (KJV)

Let's dig deeper into this.

19 "Now the works of the flesh are manifest, which are these; Adultery, fornication, uncleanness, lasciviousness,

20 Idolatry, witchcraft, hatred, variance, emulations, wrath, strife, seditions, heresies,

21 Envyings, murders, drunkenness, revellings, and such like: of the which I tell you before, as I have also told you in time past, that they which

do such things shall not inherit the kingdom of God." Galatians 5:19-21 King James Version (KJV)

Why is it that the fruits of the flesh are more easily discerned in the church than the fruits of the spirit? What does God say are the (good) fruits?

22 "But the fruit of the Spirit is love, joy, peace, longsuffering, gentleness, goodness, faith,

23 Meekness, temperance: against such there is no law

24 And they that are Christ's have crucified the flesh with the affections and lusts.

25 If we live in the Spirit, let us also walk in the Spirit.

26 Let us not be desirous of vain glory, provoking one another, envying one another." Galatians 5:22-26 King James Version (KJV)

God is raising up a generation of worshipers that will do things the way that he intends so that there can be a great harvest. We are in an epic time in which God is raising up the laborers. Those who are more concerned about what God says than what man says. Are you a part of the remnant? You can be. Let's get there together. Join me as we discuss the topic "For lack of knowledge."

For lack of knowledge

I am pretty excited that you made it this far. Once again God is continuing to prove that His word does not come back void. What does that mean exactly? It means if God said it, there is nothing that anyone can do to change it other than God (remind me to tell you about the benefits of repentance)! His word will not come back empty. Have you ever read the verses in Genesis Chapter 1?

1 "In the beginning God created the heaven and the earth.

2 And the earth was without form, and void; and darkness was upon the face of the deep. And the Spirit of God moved upon the face of the waters." Genesis 1:1-2 King James Version (KJV)

It is pretty interesting to me that the Earth started out void, formless, and full of darkness. Which in all honesty is still pretty accurate description of today's world. Yet, the Spirit of God moved upon the face of the waters. Kind of like looking at a blank canvas and saying I feel like there is something that I can do with this. Not only do I like the idea but I am going to follow through. Yes God is Alpha and Omega but He is also a good Father.

3962 patér – father; one who imparts life and is committed to it; a progenitor, bringing into being to pass on the potential for likeness. 3962[1] /patér ("father") is used of our heavenly Father. He imparts life, from physical birth to the gift of eternal life through the second birth (regeneration, being born again). Through ongoing sanctification, the believer more and more resembles their heavenly Father – i.e. each time they receive faith from Him and obey it, which results in their unique glorification. https://biblehub.com/greek/3962.htm

His response to the problem of emptiness and lack of purpose was to bring light into the situation. He added the very thing that was missing.

---

1.   https://biblehub.com/greek/3962.htm

He added vision. He verified this by saying that He saw the light and it was good. He didn't say the darkness was good. In fact he separated the two from one another.

3 "And God said, Let there be light: and there was light.

4 And God saw the light, that it was good: and God divided the light from the darkness." Genesis 1:3-4 King James Version (KJV)

God is showing us from the very beginning that light and darkness do not belong together.

"The people which sat in darkness saw great light; and to them which sat in the region and shadow of death light is sprung up." Matthew 4:16 King James Version (KJV)

"Let your light so shine before men, that they may see your good works, and glorify your Father which is in heaven." Matthew 5:16 King James Version (KJV)

"And the light shineth in darkness; and the darkness comprehended it not." John 1:5 King James Version (KJV)

35 "Then Jesus said unto them, Yet a little while is the light with you. Walk while ye have the light, lest darkness come upon you: for he that walketh in darkness knoweth not whither he goeth.

36 While ye have light, believe in the light, that ye may be the children of light. These things spake Jesus, and departed, and did hide himself from them.

37 But though he had done so many miracles before them, yet they believed not on him:" John 12:35-37 King James Version (KJV)

Genesis, you may be saying, all of those verses are from the New testament. Let's see if this line of thinking was consistent in the Old Testament.

"The entrance of thy words giveth light; it giveth understanding unto the simple." Psalm 119:130 King James Version (KJV)

"The people that walked in darkness have seen a great light: they that dwell in the land of the shadow of death, upon them hath the light shined." Isaiah 9:2 King James Version (KJV)

"For with thee is the fountain of life: in thy light shall we see light." Psalm 36:9 King James Version (KJV)

"Thy word is a lamp unto my feet, and a light unto my path." Psalms 119:105 King James Version (KJV)

"That is why it is said, Wake up, sleeper, and rise from death, and Christ will shine on you." Ephesians 5:14 King James Version (KJV)

Okay... wait, wait, wait! I get it! That kind of makes sense, but are there any verses that pull all of those concepts together proving that God didn't make any mistakes or leave anything out? Absolutely!

5 "This then is the message which we have heard of him, and declare unto you, that God is light, and in him is no darkness at all.

6 If we say that we have fellowship with him, and walk in darkness, we lie, and do not the truth:

7 But if we walk in the light, as he is in the light, we have fellowship one with another, and the blood of Jesus Christ his Son cleanseth us from all sin." 1 John 1:5-7 King James Version (KJV)

"Wherefore he saith, Awake thou that sleepest, and arise from the dead, and Christ shall give thee light." Ephesians 5:14 King James Version (KJV)

All of these verses come together to show that if there is error in understanding, it is not because of God it is because of the heart of man. He is telling us that light has no portion in darkness. Therefore, the good thing that he did was to separate it. God separated it because when you are surrounded by darkness you cannot see. You have no vision. God wants us to have vision. So what is the connection between this lesson and the name of the Chapter? What does vision have to do with lack of knowledge? Without vision and light; without God who is the source of all that is good and all that is evil... we perish!

I believe this is why the "church" is in the current state of division that it currently is in. We have heard about the ultimate goal which is eternity with God but forgotten that he is coming back for a collective. What does that mean? It means God does not want the drama in his house. Our dysfunction, disloyalty, and disturbing thoughts, words, or actions are not welcome in His kingdom. The invitation, the RSVP from the real MVP is only going to allow people who play well with others. Is your name on the list?

When you get the reservation and it says all white only will you decide you need to wear black and white to show your individuality? Free until 10; will you show up late and looking for the hook up? When it says no guest allowed are you going to invite your homie, friend, sister-cousin, and compadre and try to slide them in the back because you know the owner? These behaviors are not acceptable to God.

21 "Not every one that saith unto me, Lord, Lord, shall enter into the kingdom of heaven; but he that doeth the will of my Father which is in heaven.

22 Many will say to me in that day, Lord, Lord, have we not prophesied in thy name? and in thy name have cast out devils? and in thy name done many wonderful works?

23 And then will I profess unto them, I never knew you: depart from me, ye that work iniquity.

24 Therefore whosoever heareth these sayings of mine, and doeth them, I will liken him unto a wise man, which built his house upon a rock:

25 And the rain descended, and the floods came, and the winds blew, and beat upon that house; and it fell not: for it was founded upon a rock.

26 And every one that heareth these sayings of mine, and doeth them not, shall be likened unto a foolish man, which built his house upon the sand:

27 And the rain descended, and the floods came, and the winds blew, and beat upon that house; and it fell: and great was the fall of it." Matthew 7:21-27 King James Version (KJV)

No amount of name dropping, slick talking, tight dressing, seduction, or bribes can buy you a place in the Kingdom. If we don't learn how to play nice on earth we definitely won't be together in the Kingdom. This is why the enemy works so hard to keep people separated. Don't misunderstand me, there are some people that you should not hang out with or be around because of how they behave. There some you should stay away from because of the influence they have on you. There are also some that you should not hang out with because of the influence you have on them. Sometimes God is not protecting you from people. He may be protecting people from you.

All of this is directly connected to our heart issues. If we hate people, cant talk to one another or refuse to connect to others how do we think that things will be when we are in the kingdom of God. Everything that God is asking us to submit to here on earth are things that are a norm is His world. His world His rules. I want to see you in the kingdom having the time of your life. Let's discuss the process of how we can spend time together on our next topic, "You've got me lock and key."

You've Got Me Lock and Key

There were/are some things that I wish I would have known long before I decided to follow Christ. I was thinking, "what the heck did I sign up for?...Like literally. I got caught up in the moment! Maybe this is more than I bargained for."

"I went to church and stuff, oh Lord stuff was just heavy on me! I didn't even want to go to church but heck what did I have to lose! Then I heard the choir sing this song. All of the choir members were on it except this one lady who was off key but God listen she was sangin'...the solo! Even singing off key she sang that song like she had written it and like she had the voice of 10,000 angels. Because of that I fell in love with the song. I fell in love with her bravery. I thought wow she really loves God. Then people began to shout and my chest got tight and I wanted to cry. I was afraid to cry, the truth and pain was so much. I mean I was ashamed. I knew who I was! It felt like everyone else did too. But I felt this pull as the pastor/ preacher/ deacon whoever he was began to speak on how much God loved me. I mean there were biblical examples of women just like me that were used for greatness. Y'all the next thing I know I got caught up in the rapture of love and my feet were walking me up to this man that I didn't know. I was crying and not just any cry but the ugly cry! Because finally I felt like I belonged. And really that's all I wanted...I wanted to belong."

I wanted someone to say to me that I am welcome and at that moment that's all I wanted. So... I said yes when they said do you want to accept Jesus Christ as your personal Lord and Savior. I kind of thought by default that it meant that I needed to join the church but that's another story. That was the day that everything seemed to change for the better.

NOTTTT no, no, no, that's not what happened! All of a sudden bills came through. The dudes I had been entertaining started tripping. It seemed like the stuff that I was doing that was cool wasn't cool anymore. It felt like people could smell that I either joined church or found Jesus. I'm not even sure which one was the issue. I mean seriously things looked like my life began to go to hell in a hand-basket. I started thinking to myself, "I really don't think this whole being saved thing is gonna work. I was fine before, but ever since I got hooked up with this Jesus crew everything is bonkers and I ain't with it. You mean I come to church and cry and everything and then you decide to forsake me. How rude! I didn't even know you and all was well. Nah, I'm good. I want my old life back please."

Here's what I wish would have happened. Choir sings, I feel the spirit. PasDeaconship preaches message, I feeeeelll the conviction. The doors of the church open but then somebody who no one ever hears from because they never talk unless it's serious says, "Before you come up here let me tell you what can, will, and may happen as a result of your decision." Follow me as together we walk through "The Dor." It's time for the death of religion.

The Death of Religion

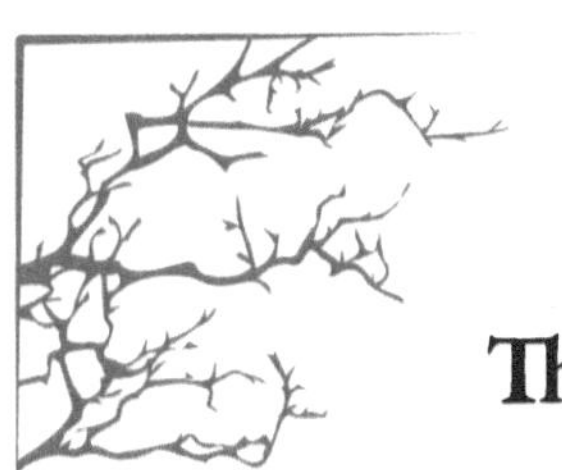

This handbook is one of many so we will call it volume 1 of "The Dor series." It will contain, sarcasm, grammatical errors, ebonics, the king's english, and more than that you guys, it will also include freedom of speech.

The truth is I couldn't tell you for the life of me why God has decided to choose me to take on such a task as educating and speaking to wonderful people like you. Seriously, by the world's standards I do not qualify. I have not nor do I ever intend to go to Seminary unless God says to. I have no college credits which I guess means I have no college education (this is debatable). I am the single mother of 4 kids (unless I get married or something before I finish this book and then well then just disregard that statement.) (Also if you are reading this book and we have ever slept together or done anything unholy or against God's law. Yeah, my bad I am sorry for being a stumbling block. No matter what happened and how many times I want you to know that the last time was the last time. I pray you will keep reading I just hope that now I am a better example for you.) Okay so back to what I was saying that whole why me thing yeah, I feel that often.

I was born to a young mom and into a messed up family. When I say messed up I don't mean it was messed up because there were issues. I mean it was messed up because there were issues and secrets that nobody wanted to talk about let alone change. As a result we keep reproducing similar choices and scraping around in darkness trying to figure out the truth. It's crazy really, it reminds me of being in the dark and feeling like you are ok because your eyes have adjusted. Some people prefer to hang out in the dark not realizing that the ability to see in the darkness means that light and separation are happening somewhere nearby. Unfortunately we stay in the dark because the truth is we are more afraid of the light than we are the dark.

19 "And this is the condemnation, that light is come into the world, and men loved darkness rather than light, because their deeds were evil.

20 For every one that doeth evil hateth the light, neither cometh to the light, lest his deeds should be reproved.

21 But he that doeth truth cometh to the light, that his deeds may be made manifest, that they are wrought in God." John 3:19-21 King James Version (KJV)

So with that little bit of information I can take you back to one of my many encounters with God. I believe God kept talking to me but I wasn't tuned into His frequency. Kind of like when you are trying to get tuned into a station on a road trip that is playing your song but you are a little too far away to not have it be full of static. One of two things happens at that point. Either you want to hear the song so bad that you listen to it anyway. Or you turn to another station that is playing a song that you can deal with as long as it doesn't take all that work to listen to it. This is what happens when we come to Christ it is also what happens when we leave. There is a verse that says.

13 "But woe unto you, scribes and Pharisees, hypocrites! for ye shut up the kingdom of heaven against men: for ye neither go in yourselves, neither suffer ye them that are entering to go in." Matthew 23:13 King James Version (KJV)

I chose this verse because I don't believe that we fully understand the importance of having the right educator. Having the right educator makes all the difference in the world. Being a well schooled educator does not mean that you are good at your job. A truly good educator considers the needs of each student. Knows that not every student learns the same way. A good educator will put in more than is required to get the desired results. A good educator learns from their students. A good educator can be found on the corner, in the library, in the theological university, jail, or even your latest Uber trip. I feel like I met great people who weren't always good educators.

Here's what I believe should have been said and what we should say when speaking to someone about coming to Christ to get to God.

"Look, I know that things are (insert emotion i.e. rough, exciting, heavy) right now. I also need you to understand the importance of the choice that you are making. You need to understand that while it is true that Christ died for your sins. While it is true that He is the Son of God. The only pure sacrifice that could be accepted because of man's choice to sin against the One True Living God. You have got to understand that becoming friends with him comes at a cost. Joining this family, entering this Kingdom will cost you. It comes with a price. When you accept Jesus Christ as your personal Lord and Savior you will become an enemy in the eyes of the world. You will be targeted by things seen and things unseen. What I am saying is you will experience trials because of your allegiance to this family. People, places, and things will try to get you to renounce who you are and what you are working to do. You will have to fight to stay in this because it's not easy. You have to give up things. Things that you really like, people that you really love. Because if your love for them is more important than your love for God it won't work out well. I also need you to understand that even with all of this you will be protected. It's like the mob. Things get handled you just don't know how. Just remember to call on the name of Jesus Christ and believe He will without a doubt go to the Godfather and make things happen for you. You've got family everywhere. Greater is He that is in you then he that is in the world. Legions of angels are in battle mode. Always watching, always ready and never afraid. Trials will come to strengthen you, to see what you are made of. What matters is that you pass the test with integrity. Finally you need to know that you may not get all the perks for this job right away. You need to know some of the rewards that you get won't happen until you get into the kingdom. But I guarantee that when you make it into the kingdom not even your wildest dreams could express what you get for your commitment and endurance."

Yoooooo! If someone would have said that to me from the gitty up. I would have been like sign me up. I wouldn't have walked away so many times. I know other people would feel the same way. Ask me how I know? Go on ask me! I know because right now there are over 9 million Greek members nationally. I'm talking about fraternities and sororities. What I'm saying is despite the hazing tactics and things that one must do in order to join people are running with gasoline draws on (for those who don't know that terminology panties, undies, boxers, briefs and the like) to be a part of it. People are pledging themselves to occult groups that require all types of things. Things that not only hurt them but hurt others. I know it, because there are still gangs throughout the United States that require and initiation of sorts and it ain't community service.

So maybe if people didn't feel lied to, played, or like you were selling a dream they would be more interested. I don't believe people have a problem working for something. I believe people have a problem working or something that they were told they didn't have to work for. You can't lie to people and expect them to trust you. Even a liar doesn't trust a liar. Not to mention that whole satan is the father of lies issue.

Here's the thing, somewhere deep down inside we humans know that life happens and everyone and anyone can experience pain at any time and on any level. So it's what you know that makes a difference in how you will deal with it. A support system. The problem is right now the support system that should be there for believers and unbelievers is quite dysfunctional and untrustworthy. How do we begin to fix this issue? We do it one person at a time.

12 "How think ye? if a man have an hundred sheep, and one of them be gone astray, doth he not leave the ninety and nine, and goeth into the mountains, and seeketh that which is gone astray?" Matthew 18:12 King James Version (KJV)

We need to start with you. I say you because you are reading this book, but in order to write this information I have to start with me. At least I do if I am truly following the teachings of Christ. The student is not above the master. No, I am not the master I am the student first which means everything that I teach I stand behind. Whatever I teach I am learning have overcome or am overcoming. I believe in following what you preach. I also believe in admitting that you were wrong if you are corrected by God later down the line. I believe in apologizing when you realize the error of your ways. That's what God meant by making the crooked paths straight. I believe in expressing how one concept and idea has matured as you have matured in your relationship with Christ and the Holy Spirit of Truth and understanding of God. In short I am saying don't sell what you won't buy!

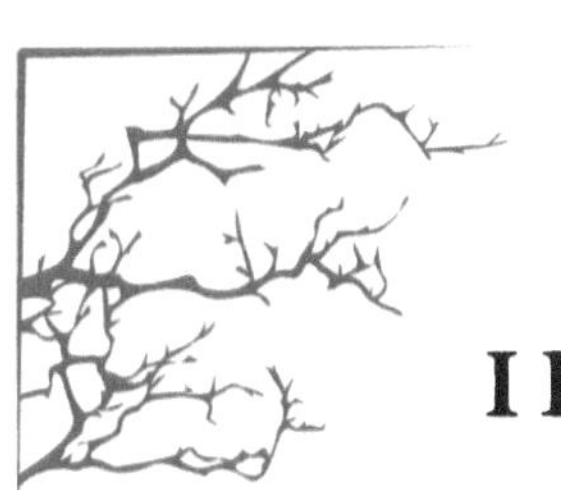

I Don't know Pastor?!

Have you ever gone to the shoe store and seen an amazing pair of shoes. I mean these things are fire. They match several outfits or even just the one you need to make your legs look cute or out fit come together men. You haven't seen anyone in a pair like this before and if you have it won't look like it will when you wear them. You go to pick them up and realize they are the wrong size. You not tripping yet because you are secretly stalking down the whatever associate must be held responsible for inventory issues that clearly must be fixed. You calmly walk up to said associate looking both happy and stern; which really means you look real crazy and a bit anxious (pycho cough cough). You ask if they have your size in the back. They do not! You ask if they have the next size up or the next size down because maybe you can work it out. You get these shoes. You at this point either cram and jam those toes or stuff them like they are a couch pillow with toilet paper. After all is said and done the truth is those weren't a good fit for you.

This is what is happening in the church. There is no space to find the shoes that fit you. You can't say this doesn't fit right or even this doesn't sound right without some type of backlash. How do you grow? How does God use you properly if you are only allowed to do it the way it is being taught when its incorrect? There was someone just like you in the bible his name was David.

David goes to see a man about a dog. I mean David's dad wants David to take his strapping strong brothers some food because they were at war and in the army of Saul. Now they weren't exactly fighting or anything like that. They were more sitting there talking about how the last thing they are gonna do is run up on this army. Why you ask. It was because they had one of the largest (Nephilim) I mean giants in their army. He was big, cocky, and in addition to that well trained. He came out to fight just one guy who would volunteer to represent the whole army. Long story short they were scared and on lunch break when David showed up.

Now David heard this guy talking stuff and he was watching until he said something crazy about God. Mad disrespectful. So David says y'all just gonna let him talk crazy?! Listen let me go holla at ya boy. Imma bust his head wiiiddddee open no questions asked. His brothers begin to insult him because they are embarrassed and a bit jealous. I mean David was the runt of the family and if you look at the descriptions of him he wasn't much of a runt. His brothers definitely did not appreciate him even considering himself stronger, bigger, or even worthy enough to take on Goliath. Even still someone catches wind of the conversation and they speak to the king about it. The king thinks he's crazy but hey why not he has heart. What he offers David is his armor and weapons to fight Goliath.

Let's stop here and interject some info. It is not okay to tell people to go places you are unwilling to go yourself spiritually. Yes it is true that everyone has their own call but how dare you ("Past- da"- responsibility) use someone else's zeal and heart for God to make you look good. It is an awful practice and it is driving people away from God. You need to repent! Okay, let's go back.

The problem was that Saul's things didn't fit David. David probably would have died trying to wear the armor of a grown man to defeat this giant. Everything was super heavy and sliding off. He probably couldn't see straight. It just wasn't working. David did what I am suggesting that you do. He depended on God. See what the king didn't understand was that David was used to being out gunned. He was a shepherd who fought lions and bears to defend the sheep. He must have been good at it because he was out there alone. Learning, growing, and thriving.

Listen... I know life has been difficult. You can't imagine why you have had to endure the things that you have experienced but I want to encourage you. You didn't actually have to endure. You could have quit? But you didn't. Now it's time to realize that your only issue is that the armor that you are putting on doesn't fit. Begin to look at what God has given you to bring to the table, the fight, the battle, the war. David walked out to Goliath with all power and authority given to Him by God and laid ya boy out with a rock and a slingshot. Then he cut his head off. Here's the other thing I want to help you with, something that helped me.

Stop being angry at people for not wanting to do something until after you do it. That is the mark of a leader. You are resentful of a gift that God has given you because you are focusing on how the enemy is moving instead of what God is doing. Don't focus on who isn't supporting you! Thank God for who is in your corner, because at the end of the day you are enough to get the job done when you are walking with God in Spirit and in Truth.

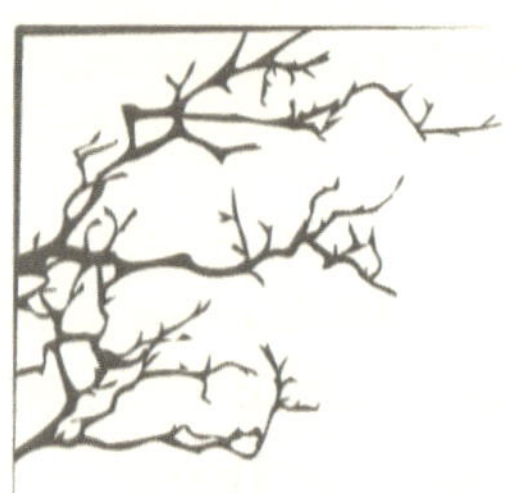

You, You, You!

Okay so I am really excited about this part. Are you ready I want to talk abouuuuuttttttt (drum roll please)....YOU! Yes boo! You! I would like to stop right now and tell you how amazing you are. You are beautiful! Let me tell you how I know, because God said so.

"I will praise thee; for I am fearfully and wonderfully made: marvellous are thy works; and that my soul knoweth right well." Psalm 139:14 King James Version (KJV)

I want to let you know how important it is for you to know who you are. One of the best ways I can show you that is by showing you how much work the enemy puts into making you into someone else. Have you ever seen the movie "Roots"? If so, you may remember one of the most notable scenes. LeVar Burton played Kunta Kinte. This scene was very graphic and intense. He was being abused by slave owners who wanted to reprogram him to answer to a different identity. A different way we can think of this is they wanted to strip him of his anointing. In the movie Kunta Kinte was supposed to represent where he had come from and how strong he was. It was attached to his history ability to overcome things of any nature. They wanted him to respond to the name Toby. A name they had given him . This is a practice that has been in place for even longer than the slave trade it was also something done in the bible.

There were four Hebrew boys. *(Now it's important to understand I am not comparing who went through more pain. I am identifying and making clear a practice that is still used right now).* Daniel, Hananiah, Azariah, and Mishael were the names of the Hebrew boys. I prefer to call them by their given names as those were the names assigned to who they truly were. However, when they were stripped of those names we began to call them what everyone else called them which was shadrach, mischack, and abednego. I know that it seems petty but have you ever wondered why we still called Daniel his name but his friends but not his friends. I believe it has a lot to do with the way we view what He did in comparison to what they did. We have this ability to move in favoritism without noticing it. Another example of this is saying major and minor prophets. Is not being called by God a major thing? Just so you are up to speed the name associated with Daniel was belteshazzar. I think that's a wack practice but we will move on.

All four boys worked for Nebuchadnezzar. They learned the language, the science, the spells, practices, and beliefs of the Babylonians. While learning this they also learned that they were supposed to leave behind who they were for the new identity that they now had. Coincidentally, you will find if you do the research that they were renamed the idols of the country that they were slaves to. Why is this important? Your whole life the enemy has been trying to get you to answer to a name that God has not called you by. Yes, you are given names from your parents but even those can be tricky. At some point we have to go search for who we truly are from the One who originally created us. God has a habit of taking us right back to what he wanted you to know in the first place.

If you came up in an abusive childhood you were probably called stupid, dumb, ugly, maybe you were called the b word, whore, and even more than that. Those were all things that the enemy wanted to rename you while you were in bondage. Now that you are no longer in bondage it is time to take the journey to learn what your new name is. The name should be attached to your character. The reason God was called so many things in the bible was because they were all descriptions of His character and nature of who He truly was at the core. The hard part is getting you to stop answering to enemy names. Our actions display to the world what we choose to answer to.

Let's look at those Hebrew boys again. They were renamed names that were associated with their new surroundings, home, and new adopted thought patterns. However, when they were challenged by the King to bow down and worship him they chose to remember who they were. Instead of what they had been called. They refused to answer by that name or character. As a result they were thrown into the fiery furnace. What I love about this story is not that they were delivered out of the furnace but instead that fact that they answered the King the way that they did.

16 "Shadrach, Meshach, and Abednego, answered and said to the king, O Nebuchadnezzar, we are not careful to answer thee in this matter.

17 If it be so, our God whom we serve is able to deliver us from the burning fiery furnace, and he will deliver us out of thine hand, O king.

18 But if not, be it known unto thee, O king, that we will not serve thy gods, nor worship the golden image which thou hast set up." Daniel 3:16-18 King James Version (KJV)

That is so dope! The faith in that is amazing. Let's go a little deeper. They were chosen to be in the king's house. They were considered to be without defect, intelligent,(genius by our tests). That means that during the exile (that they were warned about) God kept them. They then decided they would not eat the king's meat. They could have been killed for disobedience but God kept them. Then they were put up against all the other candidates that had been training with them for the last 3 years. Again they were chosen and God kept them. They were clothed with royal garb, well fed, high in status,and they never once bowed down to satan. They never forgot who they were. So when it came time to have that conversation the enemy who had been grooming them for such a time as this just knew that they would pledge allegiance to him. Surprise surprise! They made a choice. They stated the power of the name that protected them, kept them, taught them, and loved them this whole time. What a testimony.

What does that have to do with you? If you let your home girls call you b words. If you walk around calling yourself a Ho*, then you attract some of the things associated with that. It's not until you stand up and say don't call me that or tell people your name through your actions that things begin to change. Now don't get it twisted the enemy is not going to be pleased to hear you say my name is Genesis I am a child of the Most High God. He tells me to be Holy because He is holy therefore I am holy. He tells me to be pure because he is pure therefore I am pure. I AM kind I AM loving. I AM forgiven . I AM loved. I AM protected. I AM a lot of things but what I won't be is your b-word, Your fa*, Your d*ke, Your fat girl. I AM who God is molding me to be and there is nothing that you can do about it! Watch how things begin to change. You might hear things like you are changing up. Yes, you are changing up. The word instructs us to change up.

1 "I beseech you therefore, brethren, by the mercies of God, that ye present your bodies a living sacrifice, holy, acceptable unto God, which is your reasonable service.

2 And be not conformed to this world: but be ye transformed by the renewing of your mind, that ye may prove what is that good, and acceptable, and perfect, will of God." Romans 12:1-2 King James Version (KJV)

You are supposed to change. You are a beautiful concept, idea, creation, solution, witness, and answers to questions that are not readily understood. You can be the book that people will read and know who Christ is. Your actions should line up with the nature that God has given you and as a result people will see the acceptable good perfect will of God. I took the liberty of finding some verses that show who you are so that you can begin renewing your mind and answering to your God given name.

"And all nations shall call you blessed: for ye shall be a delightsome land, saith the Lord of hosts." Malachi 3:12 King James Version (KJV)

"And the Lord shall make thee the head, and not the tail; and thou shalt be above only, and thou shalt not be beneath; if that thou hearken unto the commandments of the Lord thy God, which I command thee this day, to observe and to do them" Deuteronomy 28:13 King James Version (KJV)

"For whosoever shall call upon the name of the Lord shall be saved." Romans 10:13 King James Version (KJV)

These are just a few words of encouragement the bible is filled with many more.However be warned that these things will cost you. You don't want to go around being the fake friend or the adulterous wife. The person who carries the name but not the responsibilities that come with it. Its a trade of sorts. You should want to represent to the fullest. I leave you with this in mind

18 "The eyes of your understanding being enlightened; that ye may know what is the hope of his calling, and what the riches of the glory of his inheritance in the saints," Ephesians 1:18 King James Version (KJV)

Amen.

Who Are You?

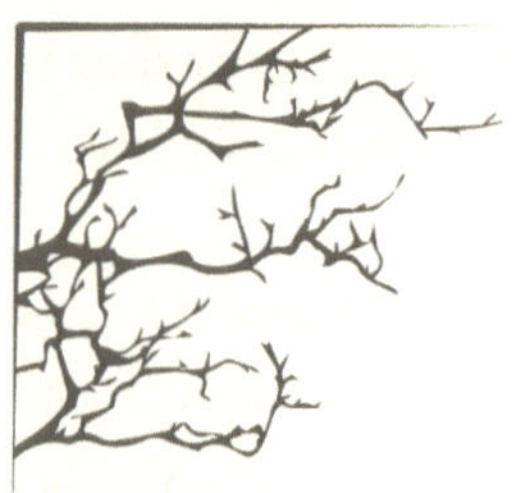

Ha! you thought we were done with this conversation but we are not, lol.

What do you call yourself? I truly want you to think about it. Even get a piece of paper and write it down. If you call yourself a Bad B, what does that mean? Is God anywhere in what you call yourself? When do you call yourself that does your attitude, behavior, or actions change? What I am asking is are you and your representative one in the same? Let me give you an example. A very popular singer stated to the world that her representative took over when she was performing. She states that if she gets hurt while her representative is present that she doesn't feel it. She also mentions that there are things that this representative can do that she could never do. She even remembers the first time she encountered the representative. So my question to you is have you ever noticed that when you respond to a certain name that specific identity comes forth?

I'll go closer to home. I had a very traumatic childhood which we will get into but not at this time. Out of the trauma other personalities were formed. I didn't realize it until I got older but anytime I adopted a nickname I became more like that description. My family members who were very close to me would call me Gen. I imagine that name was the sweet little girl with all the issues who stayed bubbly no matter what was going on. As I got older though I hated nicknames. To be honest I even hated my name. Now some of this has to do with the fact that a video gaming system was produced and kids made fun of me. As I sit and think about it the things they said in reference to me and the gaming system were sexually explicit or lewd. Because I had been violated at a very young age the two ideas connected and caused pain for me. That's why it made me feel that way.

I decided in the 6th grade that I was tired of people naming me what they wanted and that I wanted a nickname. But this time I would have control. I named myself LiL K-ozz. What I understand now is, that type of suggestion and thought didn't come from me alone. I know that the enemy was in my ear tempting me with things. Power, control, leadership. Why was this temptation he approached me with? Because I felt so out of control. I had recently chosen to go back and live with my mother. She was deep in a crack addiction. I went to church every Sunday but really had no understanding of what was going on there. I just felt really out of place. I was a young black girl in Salt Lake City,Utah by way of Denver, Colorado at the time when gangs were loud and proud. My family that I lived with before didn't allow weakness; they were fighters. So if I didn't fight... I still fought. They functioned in the tough love method. Not to mention I had left my two boy cousins that made me feel strong and loved and protected. They represented to me those traits for me. Those were also the things I needed to walk into what you may ask? To walk into Chaos.

While I can't say that I was out loud with everything. I can tell you for all intents and purposes I somehow (hindsight is 20/20) became the leader of a girl gang. My friends didn't even like each other but they liked me and that is what mattered. I was a thief. I smoked cigarettes, drank liquor, went to parties, had sex chats online (AOL dial up style), seduced older men. I also was involved in occult activity, levitation and stuff like that. I looked fine on the outside but the reality was I had become exactly what I named myself. The name the enemy had suggested. The name I decided to answer to. A synonym for the word call is "summon". That is what I had done. I summoned a spirit other than my own to cope.

Okay, storytime is over now. What am I trying to say? What I am saying is that the enemy is always trying to give you a name. He works at it through all types of venues. He uses television, radio, friends, enemies. Whatever you might listen to with your eyes, ears, and mouth. Yes, I meant that you can see with your eyes, ears, and lips. That is for another volume though. Quick interjection - I keep mentioning the next volume because some of these subjects will be broken down in greater detail. This is more of a book to get you to begin asking questions and opening your eyes.

Here's a little exercise for you to do in your time alone.Think about how many things influence you and tell you who you are? Think about the types of feelings that these things begin to cause you to feel. If you are an African American woman who hears the term black girl magic. How does that make you feel? Do you feel pride? Do you feel cocky? Do you feel vindicated? Do you think about God? Do you feel like you don't need anyone or do you feel like you are part of a group? Ask yourself these things and be honest about the thing that mean something to you. If you are an AKA, does that make you feel proud? Does it make you feel pretty? Does it make you feel successful? Does it make you feel like you are better than someone else because you joined? Does it make you feel accepted? Does it make you want to give only to people who are associated with you? Do you feel the need to do things that are God pleasing?

If you are someone one who participates in horoscopes (this is witchcraft btw). Do you feel empowered? Do you feel secure in your choices? Do you feel like you know what's next for you? Also ask yourself what do these things that I am connected to tell me about who I am?

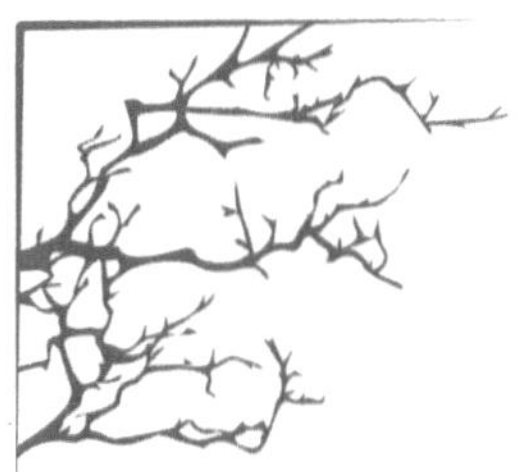

Peek -A-Boo

One of the most commonly asked questions that humans ask is," What is the meaning of life?" Except this wasn't a question that concerned me. I'm trying to think about it now but there still is no connection for me. But I realize that a lot of people are still interested in the answer to this question. I guess I was always more interested in me. Seriously! As selfish as that sounds I wasn't as torn by what life meant for someone else. I wanted to know what it had to do with me. Where do I fit in to this place? There are so many human beings. Is there space for me? My biggest question that I still wrestle with from time to time is can anyone see me?

Can you see me, is an amazing question. I am convinced that far more people ask this question than we think, but we ask it through body language. If I am unable to express myself because I have been labeled as shy (and maybe you are) then I might do something to allow my inhibitions to be dampened. Why because I really want people to see me. I want them to see there's more to me than this or that label. More to me than what they say. In a world like the one we live in, I may have to compete with what they said about me in order to be seen. I may feel that I need to prove that is not who I am. Maybe I am a person that likes people but I don't like being in public. People figure I'm an extrovert, but really I can't wait to get home. People think because they like me that means I like being around them. That may not be the case. So I may take something for anxiety in pill form, smoke form, sip form, food form to make me feel more comfortable. What I am wondering is if we are friends, how is it that you don't see me? Do you not see me crying? Do you not see me needing help? Do you not see me working on changing? Do you not see me naked, thirsty, hungry? Do you not see that I am probably a lot like the person that you just made fun of? What if I told you I am a lot like the person we laughed at? Do you see me?

For me the truth is I have often wanted to know if God sees me. Why, you ask? Well, because we get shadows of God through our human interactions. When we are children we are exposed to our parents. They feed us, clothe us, talk to us, love us; or they don't. Either way as far as our little minds can conceive they are god. We learn that they are just parents but they are our first encounter with God prospectively. If that experience is traumatic and we are not nurtured once we realize that there is a God we begin to think that he doesn't love us. We think this because we wonder why would he let all of that happen to me if he loved me so much.

This will take us into our next subject: Does God see me? Does God love me? How do I know this is true?

Does God see me? Does God love me? How do I know this is true?

Let's start with the verse,

"But thou, O Lord, art a God full of compassion, and gracious, long suffering, and plenteous in mercy and truth." Psalm 86:15 King James Version (KJV)

Why this verse? It is an answer to a common question. Why does God allow bad things to happen? When we say these things we are usually refer to death, murder, rape, poverty, and anything else that is considered obscene, unfair, unkind, or painful whether by fact or perspective. In order to answer that question we have to ask a different one. How much of what we see on earth is actually caused by God?

Let's discuss murder. Most of us will let natural disasters pass as just a force of nature that can't be controlled. That was until we realized that there are now machines that can change the weather (again for another volume). I mention this under murder because the great majority of people aren't thinking, "Why did God murder all those people?," when a tornado or tsunami hits. This leads me to my next question. When is the last time that God or even Jesus came down out of the sky and murdered someone. Seriously?! On the news you may hear someone say the devil made me do it. You may even hear someone say God made me do it. But really ask yourself, who are the murders actually happening through?

This is happening through human beings. For rape I pose the same question. When is the last time that you heard about Jesus Christ or God raping someone. These vile acts are happening through the hands of human beings. Humans being whoever they have decided they were going to be, taking whatever liberties they feel they need or want to. Let's take something not so extreme like pollution, littering, or global warming. Each of these actions are subject to those who do them. Then why do we rail against God? Why are we so angry? We are angry because he is patient. We are angry because he loves us. We have the law written upon our hearts we know right from wrong. When we say why isn't God doing something about this or that if he cares, we are saying bring judgement before it is time. We are literally crying out "save us from ourselves!"

So why doesn't God end it all right now? Just like the verse says,

"But you, O Lord, are a compassionate and gracious God, slow to anger, abounding in love and faithfulness." Psalms 86:15 King James Version (KJV)

He is slow to anger. The One True Living God when He is angry is not fun at all. We need more time! Time to repent! Because of His grace and mercy we have time to learn holiness forgiveness and all the things that are opposite of what this world teaches us. What we consider God being hateful in fact is actually God loving us. We must realize that we are the major cause of the whole of our problems and begin to repent...

Let's get into the next verse that discusses God's love,

27 "So God created man in his own image, in the image of God created he him; male and female created he them." Genesis 1:27 King James Version (KJV)

Why is this love? I believe it is because if we are made in His image we have hope. The truth is God is mature, lacking in nothing, honest, humble. In fact if you think about the things that God asked us to do you will see He already took care of those things. They are already embedded in His character. He is literally asking you to become exactly who you were meant to be and giving you time to become just that. This is something to rejoice over.

13 "For, brethren, ye have been called unto liberty; only use not liberty for an occasion to the flesh, but by love serve one another.

14 For all the law is fulfilled in one word, even in this; Thou shalt love thy neighbour as thyself." Galatians 5:13-14 King James Version (KJV)

How does this tie into what we have been speaking about? This statement requires accountability. Remember how we discussed the error in this world coming through the hands of man. In this verse God is confirming that the power that he has endowed us with can be used to do great things or it can tear things up. We should not use the power that is within us for evil. We should not let the creative power that we have, be used to satisfy our own sinful nature. It was supposed to be used to protect, build, and grow not the opposite. Because we listen to all the self talk about not needing anyone we are seeing the outcome of self indulgence. A world begging for God to come end the suffering! If we are the cause of suffering, what are we asking God to come and end?

What are some other ways that God expresses his love for us. How do we know that he loves us.

"But love ye your enemies, and do good, and lend, hoping for nothing again; and your reward shall be great, and ye shall be the children of the Highest: for he is kind unto the unthankful and to the evil." Luke 6:35 King James Version (KJV)

This is an excellent verse! God isn't asking you to do anything he hasn't done or wouldn't do. This means that when He says love your enemies, He already loved His. When He says do good to your enemies. He already did good to His. When God says lend to them without expecting anything back. He has that covered. How do we know this? We know because of this verse:

"But God commendeth his love toward us, in that, while we were yet sinners, Christ died for us." Romans 5:8 King James Version (KJV)

You are/were God's enemy that He did good to. God lent His son to you while we were yet sinners. He did this expecting to get nothing in return. While we are instructed to give without expectation we don't plant without desiring to see a harvest. We are supposed to look to God for our harvest. What that harvest looks like is will be for everyone. Let's say I have 200 seeds. When I plant them I may find that I don't get a return off of those seeds. This could be because of weather, or nature. Whatever the reason I am unable to determine what I should receive based off of what I put in. On the other hand there is also the possibility that I can receive 10, 20, 100 times the amount of seeds I planted. They key is to be thankful in all things. Don't be so attached to your seeds that if you don't get what you imagine you should it changes you into someone who only seeks to satisfy the flesh. This really is how the enemy gets us! He takes the focus off of what is really important. When God sent His son to die for our sins He did so knowing that there would be many so self involved that they would never choose to be with Him. He also knew this when he created the angels who had free will. He knew that whatever the harvest would be it would be what was best and that is what he is waiting on the Great Harvest. He is waiting for you. What a loving God.

So then how do we respond to this love? If we indeed say we love we do it like this.

"He hath shewed thee, O man, what is good; and what doth the Lord require of thee, but to do justly, and to love mercy, and to walk humbly with thy God?" Micah 6:8 King James Version (KJV)

It is absolutely amazing how perfect God is. Even in the things we perceive to be in error, God continues to confound the wise with the simple. As I stated before this handbook is created to give you information that I wish that I would have had sooner in my walk with God through Jesus Christ that is empowered by the Holy Spirit. So the deeper stuff we will go into at another time.

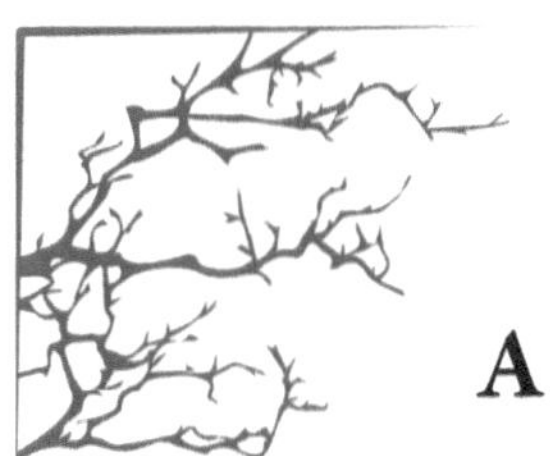

A Sinny Sin Sin, LOL!

Let's see. We have talked about God. We have talked about being off track. We have talked about God some more. We talked about Jesus. We have discussed name calling. Ohhhh I know repentance, yea yea yea this part is pretty important as well.

Okay transparent moment. I wrote something last night but when I looked at it this morning I didn't like it. It was way too formal and didn't really explain the experience. It wasn't led by the Holy Spirit and that matters because only what we do for Christ will last. I used to believe that repentance meant the same thing as forgiveness. I thought of God like a lottery. You win some you lose some. But all in all God is an okay guy and you will end up where you are supposed to because he loves you very much no matter what you do. There is some truth to that. The part about him loving you no matter what, that part is true. He loves us even while we are still in our sins. BUT HE STILL HATES SIN. I can't talk about repentance without first discussing sin.

So what is sin really? By definition sin is simply missing the mark. That is a very broad explanation right. Why is it so difficult for us to understand sin? It is difficult because humanity has the tendency to base missing the mark on their own mark and not Gods. Let's look at this a little deeper.

Most human's "mark" is initially based upon the ethics that were taught or were not taught in the place that they were raised. Because of this perceptions change the litmus test for what missing the mark means. If I have seen and experienced physical abuse all my life I may decide that my mark is simply not physically assaulting people. I may not be aware of the abuse that I experienced showing its ugly head in my speech. I begin to abuse emotionally, mentally, and spiritually. I don't feel I have missed the mark because my mark is physical abuse and nothing else.

If I grew up in a household where I was exposed to prejudice and heard and saw how this affected others then I may tell myself that I will not do those things. I figure that if I make friends with a few people from other races I am now different then what I have seen.. That becomes my mark. So when I say racist things or think racist things I am still oblivious to my error. This is because it is not error to me. I am friends with the "enemy" that makes me good in the eyes of myself.

Here's the issue with that line of thinking. The mark that distinguishes between sin holiness has nothing to do with your test. Your experience or your good or bad morals play no role in the deciding factor.. Sin is based upon God's compass. His standards and His thoughts and ways are the scale that make the final judgement. He is the determination for what the mark is! There are two places that I can think of right now that clearly explain the Lord's mark regarding sin. Exodus 20 which gives us a list of the Ten commandments.

I feel like when you come to God you should be given a cute little list with these written on them you know just so you know them. You can't imagine how long it took me to realize I don't actually know the 10 commandments. Seriously! Like turning it into a game with my kids so we can see if we even know what God wants let alone requires. It was a huge eye opener. A bit scary and funny. Like when a friend jumps out from behind a bush. You feel like whew thank God it was you but you both know they almost got slapped. So if you didn't get your honorary list when you accepted the call, or if you plan to accept it while reading this handbook here is your complimentary gift called the 10 commandments.

20 "And God spake all these words, saying,

2 I am the Lord thy God, which have brought thee out of the land of Egypt, out of the house of bondage.

3 Thou shalt have no other gods before me.

4 Thou shalt not make unto thee any graven image, or any likeness of any thing that is in heaven above, or that is in the earth beneath, or that is in the water under the earth.

5 Thou shalt not bow down thyself to them, nor serve them: for I the Lord thy God am a jealous God, visiting the iniquity of the fathers upon the children unto the third and fourth generation of them that hate me;

6 And shewing mercy unto thousands of them that love me, and keep my commandments.

7 Thou shalt not take the name of the Lord thy God in vain; for the Lordwill not hold him guiltless that taketh his name in vain.

8 Remember the sabbath day, to keep it holy.

9 Six days shalt thou labour, and do all thy work:

10 But the seventh day is the sabbath of the Lord thy God: in it thou shalt not do any work, thou, nor thy son, nor thy daughter, thy manservant, nor thy maidservant, nor thy cattle, nor thy stranger that is within thy gates:

11 For in six days the Lord made heaven and earth, the sea, and all that in them is, and rested the seventh day: wherefore the Lord blessed the sabbath day, and hallowed it.

12 Honour thy father and thy mother: that thy days may be long upon the land which the Lord thy God giveth thee.

13 Thou shalt not kill.

14 Thou shalt not commit adultery.

15 Thou shalt not steal.

16 Thou shalt not bear false witness against thy neighbour.

17 Thou shalt not covet thy neighbour's house, thou shalt not covet thy neighbour's wife, nor his manservant, nor his maidservant, nor his ox, nor his ass, nor any thing that is thy neighbour's.

18 And all the people saw the thunderings, and the lightnings, and the noise of the trumpet, and the mountain smoking: and when the people saw it, they removed, and stood afar off.

19 And they said unto Moses, Speak thou with us, and we will hear: but let not God speak with us, lest we die.

20 And Moses said unto the people, Fear not: for God is come to prove you, and that his fear may be before your faces, that ye sin not." Exodus 20:1-20 King James Version (KJV)

This is the blueprint for the "mark". I know we have tons of laws (man made) but I am always tickled by the fact that we don't realize all those laws can be summed up in these ten. Simply put, satan is called the father of lies. We are told he comes to steal, kill, and destroy. So anything that is a lie (knowingly or unknowingly omission or out right), anything that falls under steal, kill, and destroy is a whole problem. There is another statement that brings everything close to home with God's standards

34 "But when the Pharisees had heard that he had put the Sadducees to silence, they were gathered together.

35 Then one of them, which was a lawyer, asked him a question, tempting him, and saying,

36 Master, which is the great commandment in the law?

37 Jesus said unto him, Thou shalt love the Lord thy God with all thy heart, and with all thy soul, and with all thy mind.

38 This is the first and great commandment.

39 And the second is like unto it, Thou shalt love thy neighbour as thyself.

40 On these two commandments hang all the law and the prophets." Matthew 22:34- 40 King James Version (KJV)

It is not enough to the know the will of God. You have to do the will of God in love. If you fail to do anything in love you are wasting your time. It's like the gift that you offer but do it while spitting on someone. No one wants to experience that. When you half halfheartedly do anything, God doesn't accept that. If you are unsure of this as a fact think about the story of Cain and Abel. Both of them brought gifts to God. God only accepted one because it was given from a full heart. The other brother brought an offering but he didn't have his heart completely in it. God basically said oh that's nice but I don't want it. I'll tell you what, in the future, just make sure that you give it with your whole heart.

God told him that He would wait. Why do I say God is willing to wait or give grace? It is because Cain's gift was a harvest. That means that he wouldn't be able to bring another gift until it was time for another harvest. Until the next batch of whatever he was planting came up. How else do we know that just anything isn't accepted?

13 "Though I speak with the tongues of men and of angels, and have not charity, I am become as sounding brass, or a tinkling cymbal.

2 And though I have the gift of prophecy, and understand all mysteries, and all knowledge; and though I have all faith, so that I could remove mountains, and have not charity, I am nothing.

3 And though I bestow all my goods to feed the poor, and though I give my body to be burned, and have not charity, it profiteth me nothing." 1 Corinthians 13:1-3 King James Version (KJV)

This is a profound concept to me. It shows that there has to be a heart change. As a person who was super raggedy I can tell you I didn't understand this. I know I didn't understand it because I kept trying to do what I thought was right instead of having and understanding on what was righteous. Those are not the same thing. Being right and being righteous are not the same thing. We have been taught to be right instead of righteous. Rather than walk away from a fight if we can which is righteous. We would rather start a fight to prove that we are right. God is not interested in how you look to others, he is concerned about what's really going on when you are alone. The things that you think of, talk about, write down, and imagine whether you speak them out loud or not. The stuff that goes on when no other human can see you. That changes things.

Who are you when no one is around? Are you a gossiper or jealous person? Are you a stalker? Are you depressed and crying? Are you a liar? Are you a thief? Who are you when your mask is off?

I Said I Was Sorry

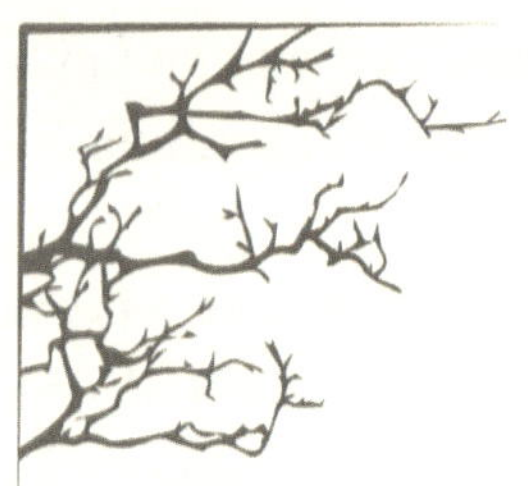

Now it's is time to discuss repentance. Repentance is more than saying Lord forgive me. Repentance is showing God that you are truly sorry by allowing change through the Holy Spirit and no longer participating in sinful behavior. Now I recognize that this can and will be debated. However, the debate is of a fleshly carnal nature, let me explain. Because of our miseducation (issa word tAday! lol) (deliberately or not) on who God is we seem to see God as being made in our image rather than us being made in His image. When you think that way you begin to rationalize sinful behaviors that you have with things like I was born this way. You think this is how I feel means it is an okay feeling. This thought process imprisons us in all sorts of ways. It attacks our lives through sexuality, attractions, desires, passions, lusts, careers.

We have a "we can't live without it" type of approach to life. If we feel it, it must be real. If I feel depressed than I accept it rather than fight it. If you believe that I can be healed or that I am healed, that means that you are inconsiderate and lack compassion towards my illness. If I feel like I am attracted to the same sex and I have been my whole life then anyone who says this is not of God is in error. God gave me these feelings and you lack compassion. If I feel like I want this drink I am going to drink it. I can handle my liquor and if you feel differently than that you don't trust me; and therefore lack compassion. In fact maybe you don't know me at all. See this is a gross error based around lack of discipline, lack of truth, and lack of accountability, and lack of love.

3 "But mark this: There will be terrible times in the last days.

2 People will be lovers of themselves, lovers of money,boastful, proud, abusive, disobedient to their parents,ungrateful, unholy,

3 without love, unforgiving, slanderous, without self-control, brutal, not lovers of the good,

4 treacherous, rash, conceited, lovers of pleasure rather than lovers of God

5 having a form of godliness but denying its power. Have nothing to do with such people. 2 Timothy 3:1-5 New International Version (NIV)

Somewhere along the line the enemy convinced us that our "feelings" mattered. I know it sounds harsh when I put it that way. I'll try another way. God teaches us about knowing him not feeling him. The problem with feeling is that there are a lot of things that we feel that are wired in such a way to give us the wrong signals. For example, the same area of the brain that is activated during and physical intimacy is the same area of the brain that is activated when you deal with pain. Meaning some of the very same chemicals that produce pleasure are also produced to guard you from pain. The point is your feelings can and will lie to you. Christ says it simple he says that the flesh knows the flesh and the spirit knows the spirit.

2 "The same came to Jesus by night, and said unto him, Rabbi, we know that thou art a teacher come from God: for no man can do these miracles that thou doest, except God be with him.

3 Jesus answered and said unto him, Verily, verily, I say unto thee, Except a man be born again, he cannot see the kingdom of God.

4 Nicodemus saith unto him, How can a man be born when he is old? can he enter the second time into his mother's womb, and be born?

5 Jesus answered, Verily, verily, I say unto thee, Except a man be born of water and of the Spirit, he cannot enter into the kingdom of God.

6 That which is born of the flesh is flesh; and that which is born of the Spirit is spirit.

7 Marvel not that I said unto thee, Ye must be born again." John 3:2-7 King James Version (KJV)

Flesh and spirit don't mix. If you are unwilling to repent from your feelings than you are going to run into issues. Most people get really upset at this truth. They ask questions like, "what am I supposed to do just ignore how I feel?" The truth is God doesn't require you to ignore theses desires and impulses. He requires you to stop them as He teaches you a new way of living, thinking, breathing. Unless you be born again you can not enter into the kingdom of heaven. Let's talk about being born again.

When a child is born (if everything develops properly) they are born with certain things within that they will use later even though they are children now. Girls are born with eggs in their ovaries at infant age. These obviously are to be used for later but they are there no less. Children are born with nerves and nerve endings. Children have the ability to experience pain as well as the ability to experience pleasure. If a child is exposed to inappropriate pleasure at a young age it does not mean that the body does not recognize this and give off a sensation or a feeling. It is now up to the adult or "Shepherd" to teach the child what they should know about age appropriate behaviors. We do this despite how the body and emotions of the child may feel. The goal is rehabilitation or (um uh clears throat) repentance, healing. I know that you may be tempted to say that is example is extreme but I dare you to think about the ramifications that lack of rehabilitation or repentance produces.

If an infant is not taught to repent of certain behaviors that they are taught through the inappropriate action then it is very likely that the child will associate this action with something that is an appropriate behavior. Without correction there is no understanding of sin. While it is possible that later on in life this child who will become an adult may learn through others outside of their circle of influence that these are not appropriate actions for a child (or unmarried adult). It is also safe to say that an action that is not corrected in most cases becomes a repeated action. It can show up whether in public or private.

We have to have the law written upon our hearts. This requires a great deal of accountability. Accountability, true accountability involves a great deal of truth. You cannot experience repentance if you are unwilling to be honest. This is why some people are alright with going into a box and telling a stranger their sins rather than apologize to the people you have wronged (whether they know it or not). We prefer to say "forgive me lord" over admitting, "I have done wrong and I won't do it again." So why is it so hard?

One reason is that sometimes we are not really sorry. We may do the same thing again if we have the opportunity or reason. If you make me mad again I may cheat on you again. If I get stressed I may get drunk again. If you lie to me I may beat you again. If no one is around I may touch you inappropriately again. Another reason is because we are afraid of the consequences. Consequences don't always look life life sentences in prison. Sometimes the consequence for some people is them feeling like they can no longer do their own hearts desires. Other times people are concerned about how people will respond to them after they know the truth. It can be scary to face the truth because you never know how another person may respond. I recently saw a horrible article that said a man caught his wife cheating. He murdered her and went to the police station. One of you readers may be thinking, "oh my goodness that is why you keep your mouth shut!" Another reader may think, "she got what she deserved." The bottom line is we cannot determine how one person will react to being told the truth. We would rather not risk taking any losses whatsoever. However in doing so we put ourselves against God to protect ourselves. Two verses come to mind.

"And fear not them which kill the body, but are not able to kill the soul: but rather fear him which is able to destroy both soul and body in hell." Matthew 10:28 King James Version (KJV)

The other is:

"Whosoever shall seek to save his life shall lose it; and whosoever shall lose his life shall preserve it." Luke 17:33 King James Version (KJV)

Do you now see how God deals with feelings ? God doesn't believe it is okay for you to save your behind by hurting someone else. Think about something that is considered small in the grand scheme of things like sharing a meme. Let's imagine that this particular meme had a picture of another human in a very humiliating situation. Let's imagine that the bottom of the meme says caption this. This meme goes viral and eventually gets back to the person that was in the picture. Hundreds of thousands of people commented on this meme. People all over the world lol'd, reshared, and tagged others in it. Others continue to remake the meme while never truly considering that there is someone else in the picture. There is a real person in that picture. Let's imagine this person goes and kills themselves as a result of the pressure and having no real support. Sad right. I pray that this moves your heart and causes you to repent. If it doesn't I want you to imagine this person being someone that you love. Again, I say I pray that this moves your heart and causes you to repent.

Why? Well there are several reasons. First being, our disgusting minds often function from a perspective of favoritism. We have concern for teens who are bullied but don't pay attention to the adults that are bullied. Some of these bullies were bullied as teens and now do the same thing to others. We don't care as much about the life of someone that we are not attracted to. We don't cry as hard for the child that was kidnapped if they don't look like the culture or upbringing that we are used to. We at our core can be very ugly. The fact that we think that our entertainment, laughs, and feelings matter more than those of the person we are assaulting shows that we need Jesus. The fact that we feel that the person who experiences pain at our hands or at the hands of others shows that this person is weak or needs to grow a thicker skin is really upsetting. Especially when you realize in some homes the way that parents teach their children to deal with this is by inflicting the same type of pain that they will experience in the world in there home.They feel like this will make them for whatever may come. I understand why people think the way they think but being right and being righteous are not the same thing.

"There is a way which seemeth right unto a man, but the end thereof are the ways of death." Proverbs 14:12 King James Version (KJV)

Without being shown that we have error we can not begin to change things. Saying forgive me is not the answer. Showing fruits worthy of repentance is how you do it. Turning away from the act, thoughts, lifestyles altogether. This is what God honors and makes promises contingent on.

"If my people, which are called by my name, shall humble themselves, and pray, and seek my face, and turn from their wicked ways; then will I hear from heaven, and will forgive their sin, and will heal their land." 2 Chronicles 7:14 King James Version (KJV)

"He that covereth his sins shall not prosper: but whoso confesseth and forsaketh them shall have mercy." Proverbs 28:13 King James Version (KJV)

"Repent ye therefore, and be converted, that your sins may be blotted out, when the times of refreshing shall come from the presence of the Lord." Acts 3:19 King James Version (KJV)

"The Lord is not slack concerning his promise, as some men count slackness; but is longsuffering to us-ward, not willing that any should perish, but that all should come to repentance." 2 Peter 3:9 King James Version (KJV)

"Draw nigh to God, and he will draw nigh to you. Cleanse your hands, ye sinners; and purify your hearts, ye double minded." James 4:8 King James Version (KJV)

And finally this verse!

"For I have no pleasure in the death of him that dieth, saith the Lord God: wherefore turn yourselves, and live ye." Ezekiel 18:32 King James Version (KJV)

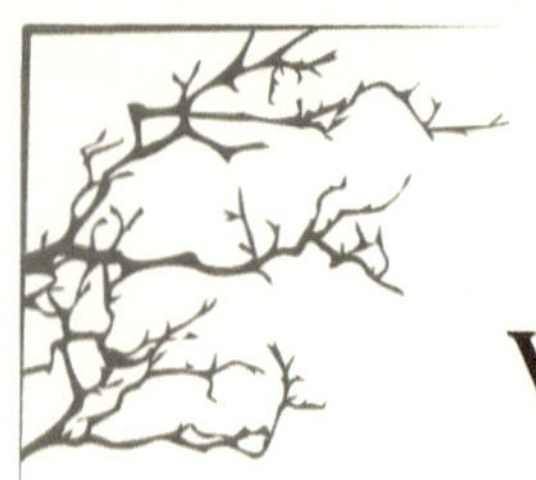

What Do I Do Now?

It is imperative we understand that although God's word shows how gracious He is there is a double entendre of sorts. You need to understand that failure to repent is death says the Sovereign Lord. He doesn't wish that any should die but the wages of sin are exactly that. Death! Spiritual death as well as physical death. "So then how does this work? If Jesus Christ came and died for my sins that means that I am in the clear right?" Wrong!

The way to access the forgiveness that is promised to you through the death of His Son Jesus Christ requires you actually believe that Jesus Christ is the answer to your sinful nature. It requires you to confess that you are in error. It requires you to believe that this sacrifice actually has the power to change things. You must believe that it fulfilled all the law and the prophets. And in believing that this sacrifice is strong enough, pure enough, honest enough, faithful enough you. You are cleansed of your sins. You are blessed with the Holy Spirit.

"Afterward Jesus findeth him in the temple, and said unto him, Behold, thou art made whole: sin no more, lest a worse thing come unto thee." John 5:14 King James Version (KJV)

The Holy Spirit will lead you into all truth. If we do things that are against God's will when we know better than we are in fact stating that what we said we believed was a lie. We are saying His sacrifice was not strong enough to make us free, to make us honest. Yes, it is true God gives us grace to learn the lessons that he has to reteach to us since we are reborn and children again. However, there is a state in the relationship where even though you are a child you are expected to mature. You will always be a child to God but you still need to grow.

"When I was a child, I spake as a child, I understood as a child, I thought as a child: but when I became a man, I put away childish things." 1 Corinthians 13:11 King James Version (KJV)

Think of it this way. Let's say you are an infant. As an infant the capabilities that you have are very modest. Especially if you are not born fully developed, or if you were born under extenuating circumstances that make it difficult to thrive. You begin to grow and get stronger. You begin to gain an understanding of things that are being taught to you. However you are expected to do certain things even as an infant. As an infant you are expected to learn very quickly to suckle so that you can eat. If you lack this function or fail to catch on properly there is a concern for health. If you don't eat you will starve. If you starve you will die. As an infant when you eat or drink, you are expected to poop or pee. The lack of these behaviors is a sign that something is incorrect and not going right in the digestive tract. If you are ingesting food and drink and not excreting waste then you can become ill. All the waste that is supposed to leave is stuck in your body. Not only does threaten to poison your system, but it takes up space for the things that are supposed to come to give you nutrients.

When basic things are not working it is reported to someone who is in a better position to figure out what is going wrong with the infant. This person begins the process to correct the errors until the infant is able to do these things on their own. Time goes on. The error is corrected and the infant begins to grow. The person in authority is paying attention to make sure the now toddler is still healthy. They are also watching to ensure that the toddler learns new lessons that line up with his or her new capabilities. As an infant it doesn't make sense to teach you to not put your hand in the electrical plug because you can't get to it. It doesn't make sense to put more on you than you can bear when you begin crawling because you still don't quite understand. Instead plastic caps are placed in the sockets and you are redirected every time you attempt to get to them. You are redirected so you can understand the error in what you are trying to do. So that you can understand the dangers.

You need to know that this new freedom to roam around on your own and explore can be dangerous if you end up in the wrong place. If you are in places where you shouldn't be there are other opportunities that you can get into that can hurt you. As a toddler you now clearly understands that the electrical socket can harm you if you stick something in it that doesn't belong. At this point you have learned that you shouldn't touch the plug because you aren't mature enough to deal with electricity on your own. If you become disobedient there are consequences that you may experience. The consequences of disobedience are present whether there is someone there to tell you not to error or not. The electrical socket doesn't disappear. It is still flowing with an electrical current because that is its nature. You are faced with a decision. Do you stick something in the socket that doesn't belong or leave it alone.

So let me interject here - some of us have a tendency to feel the parent who knows that you are curious but doesn't put in the cap is at fault if you get electrocuted. That is error it is important to have accountability in all things. This is the same mindset of those who say, "Why does God let this happen? He must have wanted Adam and Eve to mess up." No. He gave a set of instructions that He clearly felt they were mature enough to understand at the time. That doesn't mean God is in error that means that man is in error. Back to the story.

If you choose to walk away from the plug then you are sure not to be electrocuted.

13 "Take fast hold of instruction; let her not go: keep her; for she is thy life.

14 Enter not into the path of the wicked, and go not in the way of evil men.

15 Avoid it, pass not by it, turn from it, and pass away." Proverbs 4:15-17 King James Version (KJV)

If you choose to ignore the instruction then you may be electrocuted. The extent of damage that you receive determines the level of rehabilitation that needs to happen. Sometimes it's just redirection. Other times it may be a trip to the hospital. For some it may be a trip to the morgue. The point is prayerfully the child will understand that not following this particular instruction can result in unnecessary pain, discomfort, and the harm that can carry long term effects.These the long term effects can be deadly. The electricity will shock whoever misuses its power. It doesn't matter who you are.

So, how does this connect to our spiritual growth? Long story short as an infant when you come to God He understands that some of us were not born into circumstances that make it ideal to grow up in the Lord. That doesn't always mean that you were abused, or in poverty. It could be you didn't receive the truth. That's the reason that He tells us that we must be born again. Being born again is spiritual cleansing and education in how to grow up in the ways of God the creator in Jesus name. We do this through the leading of the Holy Spirit that leads us into all truth and the Word of God. We all have fallen short of the Glory of God. God has no favorites and has the same requirements of everyone. However each of us are given the measure of grace that we need in order to get along in our journey. For each person how much they need is determined by God because He knows what you have been through, what you will go through, and where you are going. He gives you exactly what is necessary to get to the end of the race.

I am saying that it does you no good to compare your life, works, and decisions to others. You don't know what tools they need in order to grow in maturity. You don't know if they need timeout or if they just need a hug. God has given every good and perfect gift for the perfecting of the saints. His mission is life and life more abundantly. He is the Great I Am! He desires to make sure that you prosper as your soul prospers. He wants to make sure that you eat what is proper for spiritual growth. He burps us to make sure that there aren't any air pockets or holes in our teaching. He builds up our discernment so that we can get rid of the waste that comes in and keep only those things that are good for the soul. He even cleans us up when we aren't able to do that for ourselves due to lack of maturity. It should be known that there is an expectation of growth and that is a reasonable request. He asks that you present your bodies as a living sacrifice. A sacrifice was used to represent cleaning for the people of their sins. They couldn't just use anything as a sacrifice. It had to be without blemish. A first fruit . I am saying when He is asking you to be a living sacrifice it means you need to be cleaned according to his standards. Fit for his glory. It means that you have to be set apart. You must be set apart in your words, deeds, actions, and even your thoughts. For what you produce in you heart will be reproduced in your actions. You will always be a child of God. But just like any household you have the choice on whether or not you want to abide by the rules of that house. If you obey the things that God has asked you are welcome to stay. It requires obedience.

33 "Little children, yet a little while I am with you. Ye shall seek me: and as I said unto the Jews, Whither I go, ye cannot come; so now I say to you.

34 A new commandment I give unto you, That ye love one another; as I have loved you, that ye also love one another.

35 By this shall all men know that ye are my disciples, if ye have love one to another." John 13:33-35 King James Version (KJV)

15 "If ye love me, keep my commandments.

16 And I will pray the Father, and he shall give you another Comforter, that he may abide with you for ever;

17 Even the Spirit of truth; whom the world cannot receive, because it seeth him not, neither knoweth him: but ye know him; for he dwelleth with you, and shall be in you.

18 I will not leave you comfortless: I will come to you." John 14: 15-18 King James Version (KJV)

And finally this verse.

28 "And now, little children, abide in him; that, when he shall appear, we may have confidence, and not be ashamed before him at his coming.

29 If ye know that he is righteous, ye know that every one that doeth righteousness is born of him." 1 John 2:28-29 King James Version (KJV)

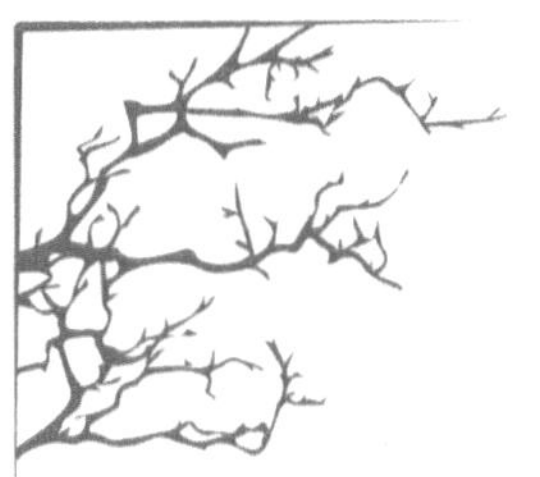

The Big Bad Wolf

Is anyone still with me? We are actually almost done! It is God's will that this book not have too much information all in at once. It's a lot to conquer. But I am excited to say you made it this far and you have plenty of material to work with.

Time to address the elephant in the room. The enemy. You've been properly introduced to him your whole life. In fact the truth is most of us know of satan and his devices more than we know about God the Father, Jesus the Son, and the Holy Spirit which is the Spirit of Truth. I have no intention of bombarding you with who satan is because in coming to Christ my guess is that you know him already. He's a liar the father of lies. He wants to steal, kill, and destroy. He runs with a team of beings that want the same thing. He has power over those that give it to him.

I have an issue with most forms of spiritual warfare. Some of the books that teach about it resembles old witchcraft books and look like it to with the displays of gauntlets and relics. The prayers sound more like spells and require you to call upon the names of demons which sounds like summoning them to me. This opens up all manner of darkness that can be discouraging. I believe a lot of the people seeking God are not free because they are practicing witchcraft unaware. I want to leave you with this information. There is nothing on this earth or that has ever been or will ever be stronger than the one True Living God. This is the God that you have decided to make your personal Lord and Savior. You have entered into the protection of the Most High God. Jesus spent the majority of his time talking about His Father and how correction will bring about change.

We are asked to believe and know that when we resist the devil he will flee. Unfortunately we don't know how to resist him, so we feel defeated. The other part of that passage says to submit yourselves into the Lord. In fact if you think about it God is only asking you to do the opposite of what you were doing. When we walked with satan we resisted God. We didn't read his word. We didn't want to understand. We didn't want to spend time with him or anything that would bring him into our lives. When we submitted to satan the presence of God was not reachable. Well the same applies if you stop doing the things that satan is pleased with. You will begin to see the things that God is pleased with. You will begin to understand the truth when you make it your desire to stay away from lies. Darkness and light cannot dwell together.

I will go into more details regarding all the subjects that we have spoken about in other volumes but I believe the major things have been provided to help make your transition into the kingdom much smoother. Finally please understand , YOU CANNOT GET TO GOD WITHOUT JESUS AND YOU CAN'T BE SUCCESSFUL WITHOUT THE HOLY SPIRIT LEADING YOU INTO ALL TRUTH.

"For God so loved the world that he gave his only begotten Son, that whosoever believeth in him should not perish, but have everlasting life." John 3:16 King James Version (KJV)

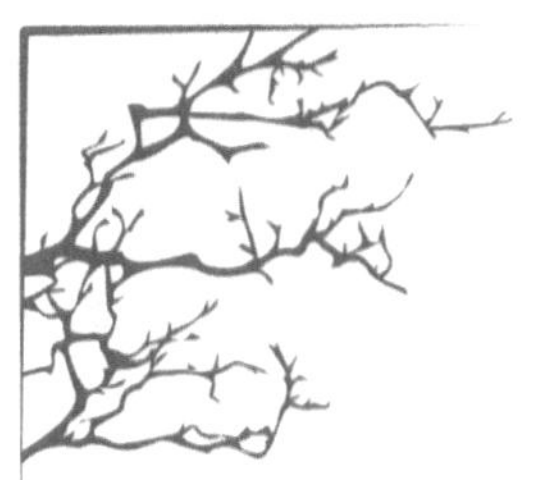

What Say You?

If Jesus Christ is not your personal Lord and Savior this is your opportunity for change. It's simple to accept Jesus as Lord and Savior. You believe that He Is the Son of the Most High God. Born of the virgin Mary and sent to die for your sins. But also was sent to overcome death. That He was crucified even though He was innocent and that He rose from the dead after three days taking the keys of hell and death from satan. You believe that he left the Holy Spirit to lead us into all truth and that he rose to sit on the right hand of the Father the one true loving God. You believe. If you believe this and confess your sins and ask to be filled with the Holy Spirit. You are a son of God.

Here is a quick version of the Sinner's Prayer to assist you if you need help with the wording:

Dear Lord Jesus, I know that I am a sinner, and I ask for Your forgiveness. I believe You died for my sins and rose from the dead. I turn from my sins and invite You to come into my heart and life. I want to trust and follow You as my Lord and Savior.

It is important that you read the bible. But be careful in how you read it. There are a lot of things in the bible that are controversial and can be very confusing without a proper foundation of who Christ is. We will talk about this in greater detail in other volumes. I personally know that God doesn't contradict Himself. However God got lied on a lot. Even in the bible lol. I would suggest starting with the books that discuss what Jesus said and letting the Holy Spirit lead you the rest of the way. A reading plan that Christ has been telling me to tell others is pretty simple. He said read Matthew, Mark, Luke, John, Hebrews, All the Prophets in the Old Testament, and the Book of Judges.

"Take heed therefore how ye hear: for whosoever hath, to him shall be given; and whosoever hath not, from him shall be taken even that which he seemeth to have." Luke 8:18 King James Version (KJV)

While I believe there are great things to read about in the bible there is nothing as important as the life of Christ. It was of him that God said He is pleased. It was of Him that God said to follow. It was Him that God sent to save us. What better story to start with! Finally in faith believe that it is done. Go at this relationship with God with more energy than you spend trying to be a singer, or dancer, or humanist or scientist or good parent or artist. Why, because I guarantee that in finding God it is impossible not to find yourself.

"And that every tongue should confess that Jesus Christ is Lord, to the glory of God the Father." Philippians 2:11 King James Version (KJV)

I love you guys. I am praying for you. As you grow please remember to teach the untaught, seek the unsought, and bring the unbrought to Christ. Until the next book talk to you later and thank you for rocking with me:)

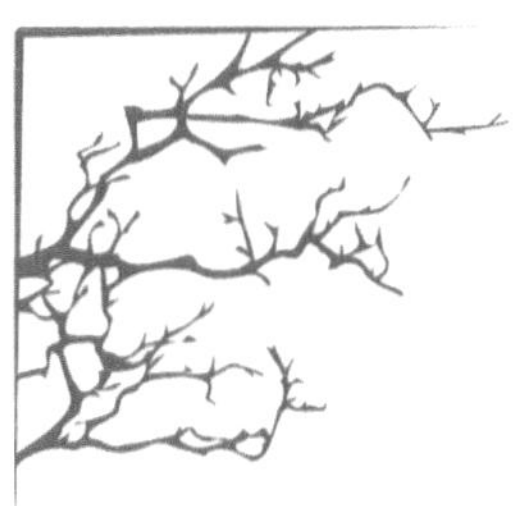

Citations

Works Cited

"2 Timothy 3:1-5 NIV;KJV - But Mark This: There Will Be Terrible - Bible Gateway." *Biblegateway.Com*, BibleGateway, 2015, www.biblegateway.com/passage/?search=2+Timothy+3%3A1-5&version=NIV;KJV. Accessed 2 July 2019.

"Bible Gateway Passage: 1 Chronicles 16:22 - King James Version." *Bible Gateway*, BibleGateway, 2015, www.biblegateway.com/passage/?search=1+chronicles+16%3A22&version=KJV. Accessed 27 June 2019.

"Bible Gateway Passage: 1 Corinthians 13:1-3 - King James Version." *Bible Gateway*, BibleGateway, 2015, www.biblegateway.com/passage/?search=1+corinthians+13%3A1-3&version=KJV. Accessed 2 July 2019.

"Bible Gateway Passage: 1 John 1:5-7 - King James Version." *Bible Gateway*, BibleGateway, 2015, www.biblegateway.com/passage/?search=1+john+1%3A5-7&version=KJV. Accessed 21 June 2019.

"Bible Gateway Passage: 1 John 2:28-29 - King James Version." *Bible Gateway*, BibleGateway, 2015, www.biblegateway.com/passage/?search=1+john+2%3A+28-29&version=KJV. Accessed 2 July 2019.

"Bible Gateway Passage: 2 Corinthians 5:10 - King James Version." *Bible Gateway*, BibleGateway, 2015, www.biblegateway.com/passage/?search=2+Corinthians+5%3A10&version=KJV. Accessed 20 June 2019.

"Bible Gateway Passage: Acts 3:19 - King James Version." *Bible Gateway*, BibleGateway, 2015, www.biblegateway.com/passage/?search=acts+3%3A19&version=KJV. Accessed 2 July 2019.

63

"Bible Gateway Passage: Acts 4:13 - King James Version." *Bible Gateway*, BibleGateway, 2015, www.biblegateway.com/ passage/?search=acts+4%3A13&version=KJV. Accessed 2 July 2019.

"Bible Gateway Passage: Daniel 3:16-18 - King James Version." *Bible Gateway*, BibleGateway, 2015, www.biblegateway.com/ passage/?search=daniel+3%3A16-18&version=KJV. Accessed 27 June 2019.

"Bible Gateway Passage: Deuteronomy 28:13 - King James Version." *Bible Gateway*, BibleGateway, 2015, www.biblegateway.com/ passage/?search=deutoronomy+28%3A13&version=KJV. Accessed 28 June 2019.

"Bible Gateway Passage: Deuteronomy 29:6 - King James Version." *Bible Gateway*, BibleGateway, 2015, www.biblegateway.com/ passage/?search=deutoronomy+29%3A6&version=KJV. Accessed 2 July 2019.

"Bible Gateway Passage: Ephesians 1:18 - King James Version." *Bible Gateway*, BibleGateway, 2015, www.biblegateway.com/ passage/?search=ephesians+1%3A18&version=KJV. Accessed 28 June 2019.

"Bible Gateway Passage: Ephesians 5:14 - King James Version." *Bible Gateway*, BibleGateway, 2015, www.biblegateway.com/ passage/?search=ephesians+5%3A14&version=KJV. Accessed 21 June 2019.

"Bible Gateway Passage: Exodus 20:1-20 - King James Version." *Bible Gateway*, BibleGateway, 2015, www.biblegateway.com/ passage/?search=exodus+20%3A1-20&version=KJV. Accessed 2 July 2019.

"Bible Gateway Passage: Exodus 20:17 - King James Version." *Bible Gateway*, BibleGateway, 2015, www.biblegateway.com/ passage/?search=Exodus+20%3A17&version=KJV. Accessed 25 June 2019.

"Bible Gateway Passage: Ezekiel 8:5-18 - King James Version." *Bible Gateway*, BibleGateway, 2015, www.biblegateway.com/ passage/?search=Ezekiel+8%3A5-18&version=KJV. Accessed 20 June 2019.

"Bible Gateway Passage: Ezekiel 18:32 - King James Version." *Bible Gateway*, BibleGateway, 2015, www.biblegateway.com/ passage/?search=ezekiel+18%3A32&version=KJV. Accessed 2 July 2019.

"Bible Gateway Passage: Galatians 5:13-14 - King James Version." *Bible Gateway*, BibleGateway, 2015, www.biblegateway.com/

passage/?search=galatians+5%3A+13-14&version=KJV. Accessed 1 July 2019.

"Bible Gateway Passage: Galatians 5:19-21 - King James Version." *Bible Gateway*, BibleGateway, 2015, www.biblegateway.com/passage/?search=galatians+5%3A+19-21&version=KJV. Accessed 20 June 2019.

"Bible Gateway Passage: Galatians 5:22-26 - King James Version." *Bible Gateway*, BibleGateway, 2015, www.biblegateway.com/passage/?search=galatians+5%3A+22-26&version=KJV. Accessed 20 June 2019.

"Bible Gateway Passage: Genesis 1:1-2 - King James Version." *Bible Gateway*, BibleGateway, 2015, www.biblegateway.com/passage/?search=Genesis+1%3A1-2&version=KJV. Accessed 20 June 2019.

"Bible Gateway Passage: Genesis 1:3-4 - King James Version." *Bible Gateway*, BibleGateway, 2015, www.biblegateway.com/passage/?search=Genesis+1%3A3-4&version=KJV. Accessed 21 June 2019.

"Bible Gateway Passage: Genesis 1:27 - King James Version." *Bible Gateway*, BibleGateway, 2015, www.biblegateway.com/passage/?search=genesis+1%3A27&version=KJV. Accessed 1 July 2019.

"Bible Gateway Passage: Hebrews 12:6-11 - New King James Version." *Bible Gateway*, BibleGateway, 2015, www.biblegateway.com/passage/?search=Hebrews+12%3A6-11&version=NKJV. Accessed 20 June 2019.

"Bible Gateway Passage: Hosea 4:6 - King James Version." *Bible Gateway*, BibleGateway, 2015, www.biblegateway.com/passage/?search=Hosea+4%3A6&version=KJV. Accessed 27 June 2019.

"Bible Gateway Passage: Isaiah 9:2 - King James Version." *Bible Gateway*, BibleGateway, 2015, www.biblegateway.com/passage/?search=isaiah+9%3A2&version=KJV. Accessed 21 June 2019.

"Bible Gateway Passage: James 4:8 - King James Version." *Bible Gateway*, BibleGateway, 2015, www.biblegateway.com/passage/?search=james+4%3A8&version=KJV. Accessed 2 July 2019.

"Bible Gateway Passage: Jeremiah 7:21-23 - Easy-to-Read Version." *Bible Gateway*, BibleGateway, 2015, www.biblegateway.com/passage/?search=Jeremiah+7%3A21-23&version=ERV. Accessed 2 July 2019.

"Bible Gateway Passage: Jeremiah 31:33 - King James Version." *Bible Gateway*, BibleGateway, 2015, www.biblegateway.com/passage/?search=Jeremiah+31%3A33&version=KJV. Accessed 20 June 2019.

"Bible Gateway Passage: Joel 3:1-12 - King James Version." *Bible Gateway*, BibleGateway, 2015, www.biblegateway.com/passage/?search=joel+3%3A+1-12&version=KJV. Accessed 20 June 2019.

"Bible Gateway Passage: Joel 3:14 - King James Version." *Bible Gateway*, BibleGateway, 2015, www.biblegateway.com/passage/?search=joel+3%3A+14&version=KJV. Accessed 20 June 2019.

"Bible Gateway Passage: John 1:5 - King James Version." *Bible Gateway*, BibleGateway, 2015, www.biblegateway.com/passage/?search=john+1%3A5&version=KJV. Accessed 21 June 2019.

"Bible Gateway Passage: John 3:2-7 - King James Version." *Bible Gateway*, BibleGateway, 2015, www.biblegateway.com/passage/?search=John+3%3A2-7&version=KJV. Accessed 2 July 2019.

"Bible Gateway Passage: John 3:16 - King James Version." *Bible Gateway*, BibleGateway, 2015, www.biblegateway.com/passage/?search=JOHN+3%3A16&version=KJV. Accessed 2 July 2019.

"Bible Gateway Passage: John 3:19-21 - King James Version." *Bible Gateway*, BibleGateway, 2015, www.biblegateway.com/passage/?search=john+3%3A19-21&version=KJV. Accessed 21 June 2019.

"Bible Gateway Passage: John 5:14 - King James Version." *Bible Gateway*, BibleGateway, 2015, www.biblegateway.com/passage/?search=John+5%3A14&version=KJV. Accessed 2 July 2019.

"Bible Gateway Passage: John 10:27-30 - King James Version." *Bible Gateway*, BibleGateway, 2015, www.biblegateway.com/passage/?search=John+10%3A27-30&version=KJV. Accessed 2 July 2019.

"Bible Gateway Passage: John 12:35-37 - King James Version." *Bible Gateway*, BibleGateway, 2015, www.biblegateway.com/passage/?search=john+12%3A+35-37&version=KJV. Accessed 21 June 2019.

"Bible Gateway Passage: John 12:42-43 - King James Version." *Bible Gateway*, BibleGateway, 2015, www.biblegateway.com/passage/?search=john+12%3A42-43&version=KJV. Accessed 2 July 2019.

"Bible Gateway Passage: John 13:33-35 - King James Version." *Bible Gateway*, BibleGateway, 2015, www.biblegateway.com/passage/?search=john+13%3A33-35&version=KJV. Accessed 2 July 2019.

"Bible Gateway Passage: John 14:15-18 - King James Version." *Bible Gateway*, BibleGateway, 2015, www.biblegateway.com/passage/?search=john+14%3A15-18&version=KJV. Accessed 2 July 2019.

"Bible Gateway Passage: Joshua 24:15 - King James Version." *Bible Gateway*, BibleGateway, 2015, www.biblegateway.com/passage/?search=Joshua+24%3A15&version=KJV. Accessed 20 June 2019.

"Bible Gateway Passage: Luke 6:35 - King James Version." *Bible Gateway*, BibleGateway, 2015, www.biblegateway.com/passage/?search=luke+6%3A35&version=KJV. Accessed 1 July 2019.

"Bible Gateway Passage: Luke 8:18 - King James Version." *Bible Gateway*, BibleGateway, 2015, www.biblegateway.com/passage/?search=Luke+8%3A18&version=KJV. Accessed 2 July 2019.

"Bible Gateway Passage: Luke 17:33 - King James Version." *Bible Gateway*, BibleGateway, 2015, www.biblegateway.com/passage/?search=luke+17%3A33&version=KJV. Accessed 2 July 2019.

"Bible Gateway Passage: Luke 22:31-32 - King James Version." *Bible Gateway*, BibleGateway, 2015, www.biblegateway.com/passage/?search=luke+22%3A31-32&version=KJV. Accessed 2 July 2019.

"Bible Gateway Passage: Malachi 3:12 - King James Version." *Bible Gateway*, BibleGateway, 2015, www.biblegateway.com/passage/?search=malachi+3%3A12&version=KJV. Accessed 28 June 2019.

"Bible Gateway Passage: Matthew 4:16 - King James Version." *Bible Gateway*, BibleGateway, 2015, www.biblegateway.com/passage/?search=matthew+4%3A16&version=KJV. Accessed 21 June 2019.

"Bible Gateway Passage: Matthew 5:16 - King James Version." *Bible Gateway*, BibleGateway, 2015, www.biblegateway.com/passage/?search=matthew+5%3A16&version=KJV. Accessed 21 June 2019.

"Bible Gateway Passage: Matthew 5:20 - King James Version." *Bible Gateway*, BibleGateway, 2015, www.biblegateway.com/passage/?search=matthew+5%3A20&version=KJV. Accessed 20 June 2019.

"Bible Gateway Passage: Matthew 7:16-20 - King James Version." *Bible Gateway*, BibleGateway, 2015, www.biblegateway.com/

passage/?search=matthew+7%3A16-20&version=KJV. Accessed 27 June 2019.

"Bible Gateway Passage: Matthew 7:21-27 - King James Version." *Bible Gateway*, BibleGateway, 2015, www.biblegateway.com/passage/?search=matthew+7%3A21-27&version=KJV. Accessed 21 June 2019.

"Bible Gateway Passage: Matthew 10:28 - King James Version." *Bible Gateway*, BibleGateway, 2015, www.biblegateway.com/passage/?search=Matthew+10%3A28&version=KJV. Accessed 2 July 2019.

"Bible Gateway Passage: Matthew 18:12 - King James Version." *Bible Gateway*, BibleGateway, 2015, www.biblegateway.com/passage/?search=matthew+18%3A12&version=KJV. Accessed 27 June 2019.

"Bible Gateway Passage: Matthew 22:34-40 - King James Version." *Bible Gateway*, BibleGateway, 2015, www.biblegateway.com/passage/?search=matthew+22%3A+34-40&version=KJV. Accessed 2 July 2019.

"Bible Gateway Passage: Matthew 23:13 - King James Version." *Bible Gateway*, BibleGateway, 2015, www.biblegateway.com/passage/?search=matthew+23%3A13&version=KJV. Accessed 21 June 2019.

"Bible Gateway Passage: Micah 6:8 - King James Version." *Bible Gateway*, BibleGateway, 2015, www.biblegateway.com/passage/?search=micah+6%3A8&version=KJV. Accessed 2 July 2019.

"Bible Gateway Passage: Philippians 2:11 - King James Version." *Bible Gateway*, BibleGateway, 2015, www.biblegateway.com/passage/?search=Philippians+2%3A11&version=KJV. Accessed 2 July 2019.

"Bible Gateway Passage: Proverbs 4:13-15 - King James Version." *Bible Gateway*, BibleGateway, 2015, www.biblegateway.com/passage/?search=proverbs+4%3A13-15&version=KJV. Accessed 2 July 2019.

"Bible Gateway Passage: Proverbs 4:15-17 - King James Version." *Bible Gateway*, BibleGateway, 2015, www.biblegateway.com/passage/?search=Proverbs+4%3A15-17&version=KJV. Accessed 4 July 2019.

"Bible Gateway Passage: Proverbs 14:12 - King James Version." *Bible Gateway*, BibleGateway, 2015, www.biblegateway.com/passage/?search=Proverbs+14%3A12&version=KJV. Accessed 2 July 2019.

"Bible Gateway Passage: Proverbs 28:13 - King James Version." *Bible Gateway*, BibleGateway, 2015, www.biblegateway.com/passage/?search=proverbs+28%3A13&version=KJV. Accessed 2 July 2019.

"Bible Gateway Passage: Psalm 36:9 - King James Version." *Bible Gateway*, BibleGateway, 2015, www.biblegateway.com/passage/?search=psalm+36%3A9&version=KJV. Accessed 21 June 2019.

"Bible Gateway Passage: Psalm 86:15 - King James Version." *Bible Gateway*, BibleGateway, 2015, www.biblegateway.com/passage/?search=psalms+86%3A15&version=KJV. Accessed 1 July 2019.

"Bible Gateway Passage: Psalm 119:105 - King James Version." *Bible Gateway*, BibleGateway, 2015, www.biblegateway.com/passage/?search=psalms+119%3A105&version=KJV. Accessed 21 June 2019.

"Bible Gateway Passage: Psalm 119:130 - King James Version." *Bible Gateway*, BibleGateway, 2015, www.biblegateway.com/passage/?search=psalms+119%3A130&version=KJV. Accessed 27 June 2019.

"Bible Gateway Passage: Psalm 139:14 - King James Version." *Bible Gateway*, BibleGateway, 2015, www.biblegateway.com/passage/?search=psalms+139%3A14&version=KJV. Accessed 27 June 2019.

"Bible Gateway Passage: Romans 5:8 - King James Version." *Bible Gateway*, BibleGateway, 2015, www.biblegateway.com/passage/?search=romans+5%3A8&version=KJV. Accessed 1 July 2019.

"Bible Gateway Passage: Romans 10:13 - King James Version." *Bible Gateway*, BibleGateway, 2015, www.biblegateway.com/passage/?search=romans+10%3A13&version=KJV. Accessed 28 June 2019.

"Bible Gateway Passage: Romans 12:1-2 - King James Version." *Bible Gateway*, BibleGateway, 2015, www.biblegateway.com/passage/?search=romans+12%3A1-2&version=KJV. Accessed 28 June 2019.

"Bible Gateway Passage: Romans 12:2 - King James Version." *Bible Gateway*, BibleGateway, 2015, www.biblegateway.com/passage/?search=Romans+12%3A2&version=KJV. Accessed 27 June 2019.

"Roots." *IMDb*, 23 Jan. 1977, www.imdb.com/title/tt0075572/. Accessed 27 June 2019.

"Strong's Greek: 3962. Πατήρ (Patér) — a Father." *Biblehub.Com*, 2019, biblehub.com/greek/3962.htm. Accessed 20 June 2019.

Utiger, Robert D. "Ovary | Animal and Human." *Encyclopædia Britannica*, 2 Nov. 2016, www.britannica.com/science/ovary-animal-and-human. Accessed 2 July 2019.

About the Author

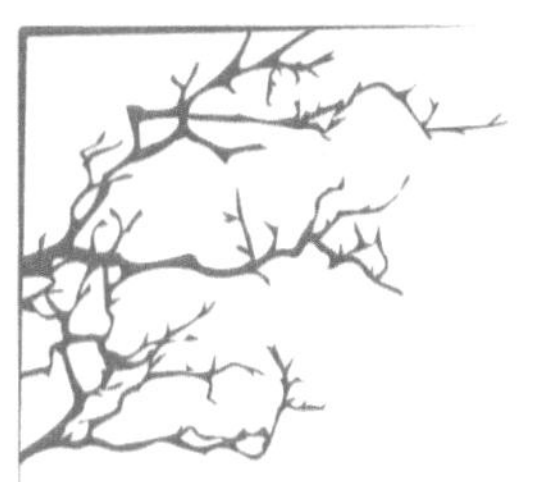

My name is Genesis Joyner. I am the oldest of 6 children. Born in Baltimore, Md. I have four beautiful children and thank God for them. I officially gave my life back to Christ on May 24, 2008. It has been one of the hardest decisions of my life. Not because of Jesus but because the odds were stacked against me. I thank God for the process because as a result I am now able to help others who want the truth but don't know where to get it. I am a lover of people. More than that just a Daughter of the Most High God. I love you!

https://genesisjoyner.com
https://twitter.com/genesisjoyner
https://www.facebook.com/genesis.joyner.52
https://www.periscope.tv/vizioninjneering

Don't miss out!

Visit the website below and you can sign up to receive emails whenever Genesis Joyner publishes a new book. There's no charge and no obligation.

https://books2read.com/r/B-A-KAOJ-MLMCB

BOOKS 2 READ

Connecting independent readers to independent writers.

Did you love *The Death of Religion*? Then you should read *Billionaire Friendz*[1] by Genesis Joyner!

Dive right in and see how your personal life decisions affect your business decisions. Can it be true that your success has everything to do with this key point? Can you beat the odds and keep your business from failing? Take a deeper look at success barriers and how to overcome them.

---

1. https://books2read.com/u/4AxrVe

2. https://books2read.com/u/4AxrVe

Also by Genesis Joyner

The Dor Series
The Death of Religion

Standalone
Billionaire Friendz

About the Author

My name is Genesis Joyner. I am the oldest of 6 children. Born in Baltimore, Md. I have four beautiful children and thank God for them. I officially gave my life back to Christ on May 24, 2008. It has been one of the hardest decisions of my life. Not because of Jesus but because the odds were stacked against me. I thank God for the process because as a result I am now able to help others who want the truth but don't know where to get it. I am a lover of people. More than that just a Daughter of the Most High God. I love you!